# CHRISTIAN PUBLISHING

# 101

# CHRISTIAN PUBLISHING

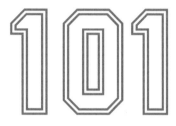

The comprehensive guide to writing well
and publishing successfully—
for new authors, editors, and students

*Ann Byle 2018*

## ANN BYLE

Foreword by JOCELYN GREEN

*Christian Publishing 101*

Copyright © 2018 by Ann Byle

Published in the United States by Credo House Publishers,
a division of Credo Communications LLC, Grand Rapids, Michigan
credohousepublishers.com

ISBN: 978-1-625860-87-3

Cover and interior design by Sharon VanLoozenoord
Editing by Elizabeth Banks

*Printed in the United States of America*

First edition

*To the best writer friends anyone could have:*

*Lorilee Craker, Alison Hodgson, Sharron Carrns,*

*Cynthia Beach, and Tracy Groot.*

*The world—and my life—is enriched by each of you.*

# Contents

## Section 4: Discovering the Breadth of Fiction

## Section 5: Writing for Children, Tweens, and Teens

## Section 6: Reaching Your Readers

## Section 7: The Business of Writing

# Foreword

The fact that you've picked up this book—and that you're actually reading the *foreword*—tells me that not only do you want to write, but you're eager to learn how to do it well. Do you know how promising that is? It takes more discipline than talent to be a successful writer, which is fantastic because it means that if you work at it, you'll improve.

Not everyone wants to work at it. But you do, I can tell.

I often get emails from people hoping to publish, asking where to start. Without fail, I tell them to attend a good writers conference. Very few take my advice though, and I understand why. They aren't sure where to find a quality conference. They find a conference but it's too far away or too expensive. Sometimes it's too far in the future, and they want to learn all they can *right now*. Perhaps job, parenting, or caregiving responsibilities don't allow them the time to go. So they don't. Plan B would seem to be reading every blog and book on writing and publishing, but who has time for that?

If you've found yourself in this predicament, *Christian Publishing 101* is the best news I can share. This treasure of a book covers everything you could hope to learn at the conferences I would recommend. Each chapter is like its own workshop, taught by a seasoned professional who is an expert on the topic. You'll hear a unique voice in each one. All you have to do is highlight, underline, and jot down your notes in the margin. Then use the "Assignments" section at the end of each chapter to flex your writing muscles and strengthen your craft. (You're also practicing discipline by not skipping those exercises and, as a I mentioned earlier, discipline, my friend, is more powerful than muse.)

I'm genuinely excited for you. This book offers such wisdom, presented in easy-to-understand segments that will give you the sense you're getting one-on-one consultations with each of the featured faculty. Writing is a solitary endeavor, but the truth is you're not alone. Each chapter will give you glimpses into other writing lives. You'll be inspired, yes, but you'll also be equipped with practical tools to take your writing to the next level.

The very best part is that this is only half the story. *Christian Publishing 101* is the next in the Credo Publishing University series. Each book in the series digs deeper into the topics most relevant and important for your writing journey. And each one will take you to the next step and give you solid ground to stand on.

The next time someone asks me how to write for publication, I'll still recommend a great writers conferences. Even more than that, I'll point to *Christian Publishing 101*. There's no better place to begin.

You're in the right place. Extra credit for reading the foreword. Now pick up a highlighter and a pen and keep going. It only gets better from here.

JOCELYN GREEN

award-winning author of *The Mark of the King* and
*Free to Lean: Making Peace with Your Lopsided Life*

# Start Here

You hold in your hands an entry way into the world of Christian publishing. *Christian Publishing 101* offers a wide range of topics and a broad spectrum of authors and publishing professionals who speak from their areas of expertise into the lives of writers just like you.

Most chapters are based on interviews I did with the professional about his or her area of expertise. I had such fun—and learned so much—teasing out the information and crafting it to benefit writers. A few chapters are excerpted from that expert's book or blog; in those cases, they did such a great job saying what I wanted to say that there was no need to do anything more.

## Creating a Writing Life

Section One explores some of the bigger questions writers face such as how to write for life, not just hobby; how to stick with the writing life; the age-old question of writing for love or money; and writing through the nos and the resistance. This is the place to see your writing as a spiritual journey and how to write from your vocation.

## The Craft of Writing

Section Two takes you right into the craft. You'll find useful information on editing your manuscript, finding the true genesis of your book, and how to cross genres. Don't miss learning how to pitch your project and how to discern your writing style.

## Exploring the Depths of Nonfiction

Writers of nonfiction will find genre specifics in Section Three, from writing devotionals to writing for specialty markets, from writing for women to becoming a collaborate writer. You'll come away with a new understanding of the depths of nonfiction writing that offer so many possibilities for authors.

## Discovering the Breadth of Fiction

Fiction writers can explore poetry, screenwriting, flash fiction, and historical fiction in Section Four. You'll learn much about research—how to do it best, rich sources—and how to write romance novels from the variety of award-winning authors featured here.

## Writing for Children, Tweens and Teens

Those writing for young readers can delve into writing for children, tweens, and teens, plus gain knowledge about board books, illustrations, and turning your books into programs for kids. This section offers a wide range of knowledge for beginning and intermediate writers.

## Reaching Your Readers

Section Six moves you beyond your book project into the ways you reach your readers. Explore five ways to reach them, plus detailed information on blogging and tracking your digital footprint. And discover the mysteries of marketing your novel and nonfiction thanks to the advice of experts in publicity and marketing.

## The Business of Writing

The final section offers you great advice on the business of writing, from publishing options to contracts, from creating a book proposal to finding an agent. This section offers a firm foundation for the writing career you're hoping to build.

Each of the 45 chapters—while full of practical information—also takes you farther along your journey via assignments designed to challenge, deepen, and expand your understanding of your writing life and the Christian publishing world. You'll find it useful to keep a notebook on hand to record your thoughts and helpful information generated by doing these assignments.

I invite you into the world of Christian publishing—whether you dip only into the chapters that interest you or that you need, or if you read *Christian Publishing 101* from beginning to end.

Get ready to learn. Get ready to grow. And get ready to write!

# Creating a Writing Life

# Writing for Life:
# Sticking to the Task at Hand

1

## JERRY B. JENKINS

Jerry Jenkins didn't start out writing best-selling novels and cowriting best-selling sports memoirs. He started writing sports stories for the local daily newspaper when he was 14, getting paid for writing before he was old enough to drive a car.

At age 16 he thought he might have to give up his dream of being a writer when he felt a call to full-time Christian work. He assumed that meant becoming a missionary or a pastor; but a wise counselor said this: "God often equips someone before he calls him. He may use your writing as a vehicle for you to fulfill your calling."

That counselor proved correct and his words helped Jenkins shape his writing goals and his view of success. He's received awards, great reviews, huge sales, and nice royalty checks. Yet those things aren't the real goals. "Success to me has always meant obedience: following the call to full-time Christian work," he said.

He works hard at what he can control: "I accept my assignments and do the work to the best of my ability. I don't compare myself to others, but rather only to my capabilities. Am I doing the best I can for the glory of God?"

His success is icing on the cake. It's still all about obedience. "Thousands have told me they have come to faith because of something of mine they have read," he said. "I know God does that work, but to hear someone say they have gone from darkness to light, from death to life, and that my writing played some role in that—well, no sale, review, or royalty check could ever compete with that."

Jenkins has good advice for writers facing discouragement. Don't let anyone else decide whether you're a writer or what you should write, and work hard. "Write from your passions. Read a lot, write a lot, hone your skills, polish your craft, start small; don't start with a book, arrive at a book," he said.

"Develop a thick skin, accept criticism only from those in the know. And remember that every piece of published writing is a duet between an editor and a writer, not a solo."

Now that you're ready to take on your writing dream with eyes on the goal and muscles at the ready, Jenkins offers this advice that ran on his blog, JerryJenkins.com, in April 2015.

### 10 Productivity Tips for Serious Writers

*Where should I write? When should I write? How much should I write each day? Should I outline? Should I wing it?*

Yes, as a matter of fact, I *can* hear the voices in your head, because they reside on a crowded, noisy street where writers of every caliber (including me) are often found—asking the same questions.

I wish I had a spoonful of sugar to help this medicine go down, but I don't: *Your daily discipline will make or break you as a writer.* Books don't make it to the bookstore shelf by your hoping for a series of productive writing days. I know. I've written more than 185 of them.

So here's a humble offering of what works for me, in the hope that these may add some premium fuel to your writing week.

1. **Write in a life-giving place.** When my writing cave was a hotel room or some other remote location, my time away from my wife Dianna was far less productive because it was so lonely. Nowadays my writing cave is 100 feet from the house, so we're together for meals or whenever I need a break or just want to see her. And when I'm done writing each day, she is my reward.

2. **Know your body clock.** First thing in the morning is the best time for me to write, before anything else has begun to cloud my brain. What I write before noon is usually my best work, and the most I'll complete all day. If you're a night person, write at night.

3. **Write rested.** Whether you're a morning person or a night person, both, or neither, write when you feel most rested. But don't wait until you're completely cogent, coherent, and inspired or you may never get to the keyboard. You get better by flexing those writing muscles.

4. **Set daily milestones.** I know how many pages I need to finish each day to make my deadline. If you keep track by number of words, fine. But monitor your progress for that satisfying sense of accomplishment—and, more importantly, to stay on pace.

5. **Tap into your muse.** Ideas seem to hit me most often in the shower. Maybe the water stimulates my brain. I learned years ago to trust what some call the Muse. My muse is spiritual, that vital part of the creative subconscious I have surrendered to God. Foreshadowing and plot threads appear as I write. I may not be sure at the time why I include certain things, but later in the manuscript, the reasons become obvious. It's important to know where your muse resides and to be able to access it.

6. **Talk out your story.** Many writers, primarily novelists, fear losing their creativity if they utter even a word of their story before getting it written. I find, however, that when I tell my story to someone I trust, I tend to expand on it, embellish it, flesh it out. Try that and see if works for you.

7. **Jump-start the process instead of staring at a blank screen or page.** Like stretching before exercise, I start my writing day with a heavy edit and rewrite of my previous day's work. That seamlessly catapults me into today's writing.

8. **Turn off your internal editor.** Once you're into the new day's writing, leave its revision to the next day and get that first draft produced. Consider it a hunk of meat that can be carved later. If you're editing while trying to create, you'll stifle your creativity.

9. **Know when to stop.** If things go well and I reach my goal before noon, I resist the temptation to try to knock out another batch of pages to make the next day easier. That's it for the day. But on the other hand, if for some reason it takes till midnight to finish my pages for today, I stay with it. I don't want to fall behind and be forced to write more tomorrow.

10. **Stay at the task.** It's easy to beat ourselves up for falling behind or not producing at the level we (or our editors) expect. The solution? Get your seat back in that chair and tell yourself yesterday is gone. Today is spilling over with fresh, pristine hours, and nothing—I mean nothing—will feel as good as actually *doing the work.* Poet Mary Oliver says, "Tell me, what is it you plan to do with your one wild and precious life?" I plan to write. How about you?

Jerry Jenkins, "10 Productivity Tips for Serious Writers." Posted April 7, 2015. https://www.jerryjenkins.com/?s=10+Productivity+Tips+for+Serious+Writers.

## Assignments

1.  Create a mission statement for your writing life. Think about your spiritual and professional goals.

2.  What discourages you most about your writing life? List those discouragements, then list several ways you can battle each one.

3.  Tell someone about your work in progress. Don't bore them with endless details, but allow yourself to get excited about your work and share that excitement. Ask that person if they have any suggestions for you.

4.  Set a daily goal for your writing. It might be word count or time spent in the chair. Record how you do meeting that goal for two weeks. Now adjust your goals to reflect what you learned.

5.  Study where and when you write best. Morning or night? Quiet room or busy coffee shop? Adjust your writing schedule and location to best meet your needs.

# The Hard Truth: Writing for Love, Not Money

MARY DEMUTH

Mary DeMuth has discovered one of the sad truths about the writing life: it's hard to make a living as a purveyor of words. "I was very discouraged for a few years; I was trying to force my writing to make money," she said. "But I had to give up that dream of making writing successful financially."

Instead of forcing the writing, she diversified by adding speaking, mentoring writers, and editing. While editing isn't her sweet spot, she does it when jobs come her way. Speaking now brings in 75 percent of her income and takes 25 percent of her time. Writing and editing is 25 percent of her income but takes 75 percent of her time.

"Be wise and learn. Don't go into writing blind; read about writing but don't just read the success stories," she said. "And be very cautious of publishing gurus, those who say if you just work my system you'll make six figures. Most of them make money on you learning to make money. Do your homework."

DeMuth's writing journey started in the 1990s—before the Internet changed almost everything. She kicked off her writing dreams by giving herself writing assignments, setting deadlines for those assignments, then making the deadline early. She wrote mostly in obscurity for a decade, getting feedback whenever possible, and reading books on the craft of writing. She attended her first writers conference—Mount Hermon Christian Writers Conference—in 2003.

There she met her agent, who sold two nonfiction books right away. *Ordinary Mom, Extraordinary God* and *Building the Christian Family You Never Had* released within a year of each other. DeMuth has had nearly 40 books published, some with traditional houses and some indie published, with a mix of mostly nonfiction and some fiction.

"Train yourself to love writing, to show up every day at the computer," said DeMuth, who lives in North Texas. "Start with a word count per day—maybe 250—then work up to a word count of 1,000 or so, as long as it doesn't mess up your quality."

She writes best in the morning, so works on the most important writing then. She saves podcasting, blogging, and interviews for the afternoon. Her advice: Find when your best writing time is and work hardest then.

When DeMuth looks back on her writing journey, she marks several key milestones.

1. Having a mentor early on. Her mentor was a professor, who had published his own fiction and nonfiction and who helped guide her writing and learning process.

2. The decision to actively pursue everything it took to be a writer. "There is no such thing as passive publishing," she said. "You have to go after it, be hungry, understand the publishing industry, be a voracious reader, read marketing books. Gone are the days of getting your book out and it magically selling. You have to become a student."

3. Joining a Mastermind Group. This group of experienced writers meets virtually twice a month and in person once a year. "It changed my life," she said.

While joining a Mastermind Group may not be an option for you, every writer can find a group of like-minded folks either online or in their community. Search one out or create one yourself.

If she were starting today, her best advice to herself would be to start a blog, give herself blog deadlines, and blog consistently. She also would have spent time learning about branding herself as an author, and would have focused on what she truly wanted to write instead of writing what she thought others wanted.

She has other pieces of advice for people who want to build a writing life.

- Put aside extras such as PTA and part-time jobs. Hire a housekeeper—let go and let others.

- Put together a prayer team of people who support you wholeheartedly.

- Attend writers conferences whenever possible.

- Take joy in little victories and its corollary: don't set your sights so high that nothing satisfies.

- Don't always take the first yes, especially when looking for an agent. Make sure jobs and agents fit you.

- Think of those queries and turndowns dispassionately. It's the wrong time; the wrong publisher; the wrong topic. "It's not emotional; it's business," she said.

Finally, settle your worth before you begin the writing journey. "Your work doesn't equal you," said DeMuth. "You're headed for heartache if you haven't settled that first."

··· Visit marydemuth.com ···

---

### Courage and Creativity – Ann Spangler

Ann Spangler, a veteran of the publishing industry, has worked for small and large publishers, lived in Michigan and Arizona and Michigan again, adopted two daughters and written close to 20 books.

Her life trajectory points to the unique joys and challenges of building a writing life. She followed God's heart and leading, wasn't afraid to step into the unknown, and wasn't afraid to try something new.

"I was pretty good at taking risks and a lot of them panned out," she said. "You have to have confidence, be a risk taker, and be driven by joy. I knew I would stagnate if I didn't take the next step."

She admits to hesitation, but not to fear. "I wasn't stepping into thin air; I was jumping into something. There were bridges there because I'd built the relationships. I took the next step and the next, not just jumped from one thing to another."

Spangler, a bit of an entrepreneur in the writing business, is honest about the writing life. It's romantic when you sign a contract and hold your book in your hands. "But otherwise it's just hard work. It's satisfying and lonely, but hard work," she said.

Marketing is part of that hard work. She wants to write and let the publisher do the marketing, but admits that doesn't work anymore. She encourages writers to build up their social media, to develop that platform.

Her best advice: "Branch out in new and fresh ways, look for more interesting ways to tell your story. And always learn."

··· Visit annspangler.com ···

---

### Assignments

1. Give yourself three writing assignments—blog posts, devotionals, query letters—and set deadlines for those assignments. Now meet the deadline or make it early.

2. How have you settled your worth? Who are you in Christ? Create a list of six Bible verses that speak to your place as a beloved child of God. Meditate on them.

3. If you're looking to make a living as a writer, how might you diversify your portfolio? Can you edit? Mentor? Write marketing copy? Write magazine or newspaper articles? List the things you can do to create income, then list the steps to take advantage of those options.

4. What roles/tasks/extras can you set aside to make time for writing? Make a list and begin extricating yourself.

5. Imagine where you'd like to be in your writing life five years from now. What decisions will help you get there? What actions might you need to take now?

# Write, Write, Write:
## Advice from a Seasoned Professional

3

DENNIS HENSLEY

Dennis "Doc" Hensley, PhD, decided to become a professional writer in 1965, thanks in part to his high school English teacher Mr. Ringle. Mr. Ringle suggested that being a clown or a brain surgeon might be an easier path, but young Hensley wouldn't take no for an answer.

He read and wrote, wrote and read. He attended a community college near Bay City, Michigan, for his associate's degree, then finished at a four-year college. He did two years in the U.S. Army, including one in Vietnam. He wrote through all of it and continues to write today. Doc is now chair of the Department of Professional Writing at Taylor University, author of 60 books and numerous articles, devotionals, book reviews, interviews, and feature stories.

He experiences the same joys and struggles all writers do. "I leap for joy when my literary agent calls and says he has gotten a phenomenal offer on my latest manuscript. I love, love, love to sign with a reputable publishing house, and I am delirious about getting a nice, big cash advance," he says.

He loves reading complimentary reviews of his books, has fun talking about his books on television and radio, and enjoys it when people recognize him. "I suppose I am as big a ham as anyone," he says. "But let me be genuine in saying there are other joyful elements to the career. The first is the impact I can make as a writer."

Doc teaches a Sunday school class with 45 attendees who enjoy studying the Word of God together. But if he writes a devotion for *The Upper Room* or *Pathways to God*, it can reach 450,000 people. "That's a real amplification of my effort to spread the Word of the Lord. This isn't just a job; it's a ministry," he says. "There's an old hymn that says, 'There is joy in serving Jesus,' and quite honestly, in my case that is very true."

A writing career isn't all yeses from publishers and hamming it up on radio and television. Saying no is painful for him. Between teaching full-time, writing a monthly column for *Christian Communicator*, speaking at writers conferences and book deadlines, he can't do everything. He has to say no to some speaking and writing requests. "There have to be priorities, and I understand that," he says. "My two obligations outside of caring for my family are my college teaching and my writing."

Doc's advice is tough, simple, and pointed.

**For beginning writers:** "The biggest mistake most novice writers make is being so terrified of getting rejected they never reach closure on anything. I've met many writers who are members of a writers' club, who attend writers conferences, and who read myriad books and magazines about aspects of professional writing, yet they never finish a project and submit it," he says.

They have one act of a play, three chapters of a romance novel, notes for a children's book, the first draft of a poem, pages of ideas for devotions. Nothing is finished and nothing has been submitted.

"These people are playing at being writers. They do not finish anything because, if they did, it might get rejected and that would mean they really aren't writers," says Doc. "To them, it's far better to act the part and enjoy the camaraderie of fellow wordsmiths than face the reality of needing re-writes and preparing second and third drafts. They never get anywhere because they don't strive for closure on individual writing projects."

**For experienced writers:** "Never align yourself with just one publishing venture. You never know when your editor will die, be fired, take a new job somewhere else, or retire. When that happens, you may be out too," says Doc.

It's happened to him numerous times, but he's always had a Plan B. He spent 22 years as a regional correspondent for *Writer's Digest*, but when a new group of young editors took over, he was dropped. He moved to *Writer's Journal*, where he was a columnist and contributing editor for 11 years until the magazine folded. He now writes that same column for *Christian Communicator*.

"I always kept a new door open in case an old door closed," he says.

His second piece of advice is that experienced writers must keep reinventing themselves.

"Publishing is a fickle business. What is hot for a season will cool soon thereafter. Knowing this, I've recreated my writing image numerous times," says Doc. "I have been a columnist, reviewer, songwriter, writing professor, investigative journalist, futurist, nonfiction book author, scriptwriter, and comedy writer."

He encourages writers to explore new writing venues (print, online, webinars, blogs, websites) and new writing genres (humor, drama, young adult, journalism, feature writing, travel writing, sci-fi). "Limiting yourself to one specialty will lead to stagnation, repetitiveness, and a loss of readers," he says.

**For every writer:** "I harp and preach and proclaim this message: 'Develop a turtle-shell hide.' Don't let criticism of your writing be something you interpret as criticism of yourself as a person. Learn to separate the two."

Doc has offered this advice for years and it never changes. He urges writers to learn from edits and critiques by more experienced writers, to listen when an editor or seasoned writer demonstrates why a piece of writing doesn't work.

"Don't try to explain or justify what you wrote," he says. "Gain from his or her knowledge and experience. There is a reason why that person is getting published and you're not."

Doc Hensley has seen big changes in publishing through the years. He admits to writing high school term papers on a manual typewriter. Now he writes on his state-of-the-art computer and uses email and the Internet nonstop. "I can write and submit manuscripts ten times faster than in the old days, and I love it," he says.

The downside, however, is that all media have become glutted. "People confuse being printed with being published. Anyone—talented or not— can record a song or write a book or make a film and put it online," says Doc. "The only salvation is that I've seen in the long run that talent does continue to 'out.' Cream still rises to the top, even in an ocean of milk."

Doc Hensley stresses to his writing students and the people he meets at writers conferences to create the highest quality material possible. He stresses the same thing in his own writing life, striving to stay current with news, trends, society, technology, politics, religion, science, and entertainment. And he has no plans to retire.

His dad, he said, worked well into his 70s before retiring from a career making and fitting artificial eyes for people who lost one due to disease or an accident of some kind. "My dad never hated going to work," says Doc. "It was pure joy for him. I felt that writing could be like that for me."

Enjoy it he does. "I read voraciously and seek interesting people to talk with and watch many movies and sample a lot of television. One day I will step down from my full-time position as a college professor, but I will continue to write for as long as I enjoy it and as long as there are readers who want to read my material. I can't think of any career I'd rather have than being a writer, and knowing that my writing serves the Lord makes it all that much sweeter."

••• Visit dochensley.com •••

## Assignments

1.  List the projects you have begun but not finished. Write down why you haven't finished those projects and what fears might be keeping you from completing them. Talk to an experienced writer you trust about the truth of those fears, then decide how you will move past them.

2. Consider the places for which you write now. What if those venues were to fold or the editors were to move on? What is your Plan B? Create a list of new publishing venues that interest you, including editors' names, requirements, and contact information. Submit a piece to one of them.

3. Have a more experienced writer, either someone you know or via a writing contest or conference, critique a piece of your writing. Answer these questions: How did the critique make you feel? What changes can you make to improve your writing? What resistance did you feel?

4. Assess how you would like your writing life to look, whether as a career, a hobby, or a moneymaking venture. Create a career plan for your writing life, including what education you'll need, career goals, even salary dreams. List the steps you can take now, next year, and in the next five years.

5. How do you see writing as part of your Christian life? Write a mission statement that blends your writing and your faith and how the two interact.

# Mission and Vision:
## Opening Our Hearts and Minds to Differences

4

## STACY HAWKINS ADAMS

Stacy Hawkins Adams was the first African-American novelist her publishing house had published when her first book was released in 2004. She's done many novels since then, and she knows there is room for growth when it comes to diversity in both staff and authors in the Christian publishing world. Diversity, she said, applies to race, culture, gender, and generational differences. Her mission is to bring the body of Christ together in its diversity.

"The first step is enlarging your own personal territory," said Adams, director of communications for a top private school in Richmond, Virginia. "It takes extra effort to build bridges."

She always wants to bridge gender, racial, and cultural divides. She had a white, male friend read her novels.

"He told me that I only had black characters, but that black people have white people in their lives," said Adams.

She also heard from white women readers saying that her stories were their stories too, but that they may not get their friends to read Adams's books because there were only black people on the covers. Now her covers have no people on them.

"This was very instructive to me to broaden my understanding," said Adams.

She also had a man read one of her books featuring a male lead.

"He said that a man home alone with his wife gone is not sitting on the bed watching a movie and eating cake. He's watching ESPN on the couch and eating cold pizza," she said.

She encourages writers to step out, branch out, reach out.

"If you are white and want to incorporate African-Americans, find friends who are African-American and ask them to read your book," she said. She offers the same advice to African-American writers, and all writers of different races, religions, and cultures.

"Build relationships outside of your circle to know people who can comfortably reflect their experience," she said.

Debate rages on whether white people can write about people of color. In the general market, Laurie Halse Anderson writes about a slave girl in her The Seeds of America Trilogy (Atheneum Books for Young Readers). "I didn't care that she was a Caucasian writer; I was pulling for that slave girl."

Jodi Picoult in *Small Great Things* creates African-American characters. "I had to stop reading and go to the back of the book [to her notes] to see how she knew all that stuff," she said.

Adams encourages readers to write about their broad experiences, which readers will see and, hopefully, begin to take those steps in their own lives.

"Step outside your comfort zone," said Adams. "It's worth the effort to broaden your readership and help Christians understand each other."

---

## Writing for an Audience of One – Stacy Hawkins Adams

Stacy Hawkins Adams is a hybrid writer. She's written for a variety of audiences—Christian and general—in a variety of genres, from newspaper columns to news stories, from novels to nonfiction. On all the tracks her writing has taken, she always writes to an audience of one.

"When you find your mission and figure out the lane God wants you in and when you write with the purpose he has given you, you are honoring him and writing for that audience of one: God," she said.

Adams was a full-time newspaper writer for 14 years, the last six years including a faith-based column for the paper. She left newspapers to write faith-based fiction, them moved back to full-time work as director of communications for a top private school in Richmond, Virginia. She's also writing a parenting column these days, as well as speaking and working on several books.

The audience of one can also be that one reader who is impacted by your work. Adams, when she announced she was leaving the paper, received all kinds of emails and letters from people telling her that the column had spoken to them.

"Part of writing to the audience of one is to be okay with the process of being on that life journey," she said. "We all have a unique path in life and a unique journey. We can pull from the lessons learned, the encounters we have and make metaphors of those things to connect with readers."

Key, she said, is discovering your mission and vision for your writing life. Find and refine your purpose, surrender your stories to God, and write with conviction is her best advice no matter what you write.

**To publishers she says this:** "With strategic thought and effort, you can make a solid business choice and a solid missional choice. This is a global world; we can help each other understand one another and we can appreciate each other's diversity and what that brings to our relationships."

She encourages publishers to understand that just about everything about publishing for diverse readers is different, from storytelling to marketing. African-Americans, for instance, experience cross-pollination in all areas of life. They read the Bible and listen to R&B music, enjoy *Essence* magazine and *Our Daily Bread* devotional. Advertising and marketing is, therefore, different than that to an evangelical, white readership.

**For writers:** "We have to be comfortable being uncomfortable. When we're stretching past what we know and our comfort zones, we're on the right path. Cross-pollination occurs when we realize we're all brothers and sisters in Christ and the more we embrace the need for diversity and inclusion."

··· Visit stacyhawkinsadams.com ···

"Write your way forward, experience life, and trust the story," she said. "Refining the process comes from reader feedback."

Her first novel, *Speak to My Heart*, came out in 2004. Not long afterward, she called her mom to tell her she'd finished the second book. Her mom died a month later. Adams stopped writing, and when a friend asked about her writing she said it was more of a hobby and that she'd get back to it sometime.

"That night I got an email from a woman in Washington, DC, who said she had moved there to be with a man who had left her to marry another," Adams recalled. "She said that she had planned to kill herself, but her mom had sent her my book and she read it; she decided not to kill herself. That's when I decided writing books was about more than myself."

She talks more about that second book. "When I got the edits back, I began reading and realized the main character was mourning her mother. The book was ministering to me and I had written it!"

**Her advice for fiction writers:** "Write forward. Sit in the chair and start writing, even if you need to start with journaling or free-writing. And keep writing. Only read what you've written to get yourself back into the story. You know it's a mess, but write forward."

**For nonfiction writers:** "Free-writing and journaling can lead to nuggets. I start from inner reflection and let it flow. Nonfiction for me felt so personal; it was an act of obedience. I started to picture in my mind a struggling person in the bookstore. I would fail them if I couldn't be transparent enough, honest enough about my deepest feelings, hurts, and struggles. That's when you hear from readers."

··· Visit stacyhawkinsadams.com ···

## Assignments

1.  How have you experienced different cultures and diverse people in your life? How have you included diversity—culture, race, age—in your writing? Why or why not?

2.  How do you think you write to an audience of one? Describe your one reader and describe how you write for God as reader.

3.  Create a list of people you can ask to read your manuscript to make sure your depictions and language is appropriate.

4.  What are your fears regarding people of different cultures and races? What makes you afraid?

5.  Read several novels written by those from other cultures to expand your literary horizons. Choose several nonfiction titles as well.

# Delivering Babies and Books: Writing from Life and Vocation

## 5

## DR. CAROL PETERS-TANKSLEY

Dr. Carol, as she is known on her blog and radio program, spent a lot of years gaining experience and healing from her painful past. She is a medical doctor, a practicing OB/GYN, and a reproductive endocrinologist. She also has a Doctor of Ministry from Oral Roberts University. Her love of theology and spiritual understanding, plus her vast experience dealing with women's issues, put her in a unique place to reach a wide audience. She wondered if she should write a book.

Dr. Carol spent significant time looking at her word bank—blog posts, academic papers, speaking notes, radio programs—before deciding that she had enough material for a book. More importantly, she studied her potential audience.

"I began thinking about what kind of person resonates with what I want to say. Who hears me?" she said. "I wanted the demographics, but also the pain points and life struggles of the people I would be writing to."

She asked herself pointed questions about her audience and her potential book. "What do my potential readers understand, know, and do right now and what do I want them to understand, know, and do after reading my book?" she said. "I spent time defining the journey I hoped to take them on."

Dr. Carol's first book, *Live Healthy, Live Whole*, was published independently. Her second and third book, *Dr. Carol's Guide to Women's Health* and *Overcoming Fear and Anxiety through Spiritual Warfare*, were published traditionally with Siloam, an imprint of Charisma House. More books are on the horizon.

Dr. Carol knew from childhood that she wanted to be a physician, but she also grew up in a troubled home. She had some deep personal traumas to work through as well as maturing to do, spiritually, psychologically, and emotionally. But that journey became an integral part of what she wanted to share.

In 2009, a year after her marriage, her husband was invited to help start a radio station, which offered her some unassigned time to host *The Dr. Carol Show*. She started a blog in 2011; she wrote several booklets ("I look back at them now and cringe a little").

By 2013, she knew she was ready to write a book. She also understood a key point about writing based on experience and vocation.

"It's important in looking at your life stories to discern what can mean something to someone else," said Dr. Carol. "It's important to make the communication about them and not me. Sharing my story can offer credibility, but it's really about the reader."

Her story becomes important only when it can address something her reader needs, she adds. "My story or the stories I share about others are the hook, but not the point," she said. "It's always about the reader."

Dr. Carol's mother illustrates the point. Her daughter, Dr. Carol's sister, had entered an alcohol and drug abuse treatment program, but her mom couldn't wrap her head around what was happening. She went to a counselor, who said, "When my son was in treatment . . ." That's all her mom needed. "My mom told me, 'I knew I was safe and understood,'" Dr. Carol said.

Sometimes a short story is all it takes for a reader to grasp that Dr. Carol knows what she's talking about and understands. She figures her stories or those of others are 10 percent or less of every chapter.

Dr. Carol knows that God wastes nothing, that he can take anything and make it meaningful. "If we make everything available to him, he takes it and makes it useful," she said. She points to the story of Jesus' miracle of feeding thousands with just a few small loaves of bread and a few fishes offered by a child.

"Whatever you have, you bring. In the breaking of that, people are fed," said Dr. Carol. "You're not ready to share until what you have learned becomes about other people; you're ready to share when your bread is broken. Everything you go through is useful and important if you let God take and use it in the way he wants."

••• Visit drcarolministries.com and defeatyourfear.com •••

## Assignments

1. What experiences do you have that you want to share? List them, including spiritual, emotional, psychological, and physical experiences.

2. Who will benefit from what you have learned? Make a chart of who your readers will be, including age, stage of life, sex, education, spiritual maturity, pain points, and struggles. Add categories as necessary.

Be careful to not make your audience too broad (e.g., every Christian woman, or all Christians who struggle with a spiritual issue).

3. Write a mission statement for your book, outlining what your readers already know, understand, and do, and also what you want them to come to know, understand, and do after reading your book.

4. List at least 15 stories you'd like to share in your book. Now write each one in three paragraphs or less.

5. Take those stories and list the corresponding point(s) you'd like your readers take away.

# Communion with God: Writing as Spiritual Journey

**6**

## SHARON GARLOUGH BROWN

Sharon Garlough Brown was a pastor and spiritual director before she became a novelist. She didn't leave those vocations behind, but instead incorporated her search for God into her writing.

"Communion with God is what I like about writing. Every step is deep and ongoing listening as I write," she said. "There is delight in the process of writing: What will I learn today? What will I see today? What will the characters glimpse today?"

Questions like these harken back to Brown's vocation as spiritual director and retreat leader, roles she took on full-time after years in pastoral ministry. It was while she was a pastor leading a weekly spiritual formation group that her long-dormant dream of writing revived. She had wanted to write since childhood, but put those dreams on hold.

"I was learning with the people I was leading what it meant to be attentive and awake to the presence of God in my life, and helping others find that presence," said Brown. She soon began to write.

She knew she wanted to write about the spiritual journey—through spiritual formation and direction—but didn't know which tack to take. Nonfiction? There were many nonfiction resources. Fiction?

"I figured the best way to tell the story was to make it a story," she said.

Brown self-published *Sensible Shoes* in 2010, though it wasn't long before InterVarsity Press decided to republish it under their Crescendo imprint, the first novel ever in that line. *Sensible Shoes: A Story about the Spiritual Journey* released in 2013, followed by *Two Steps Forward: A Story of Persevering in Hope*; *Barefoot: A Story of Surrendering to God*; and *An Extra Mile: A Story of Embracing God's Call*. The publisher also released a study guide for *Sensible Shoes*.

The series focuses on four very different women who meet at a spiritual retreat and eventually become friends. They deal with unique spiritual issues, yet are deeply committed to one another and their spiritual journeys.

"The first thing I did was pray and ask God to reveal to me one thing that happened to that woman as a little girl that relates to what her struggles are now. Nothing was plotted or planned, so it all took me by surprise," said Brown.

One day her son, David, found her bawling as she wrote through a scene. He suggested that she was the author and in charge of the story.

"But I'm not in charge," she sobbed. "I don't have control of the story."

That is one of the key spiritual lessons Brown learned through the process of writing: giving up control—control of her characters, the writing process, the publishing process, reviews, and even readers.

"It wasn't just the book I surrendered, but the readers as well," said Brown. "I would love to have a particular section in bold print and red letters that says, 'Don't turn the page until you understand what the spiritual director is saying.' But I just plant the seeds; the growth is up to God."

Reader growth, but character growth as well. She hit a wall for three days while writing *Sensible Shoes*. She didn't have a clue how a character would get unstuck from a problem in her life.

"I was praying when God said, 'You need to leave her in her pain and trust me to work in her.' He revealed at that moment that I had become codependent with my character and was trying to rescue her. The minute I tried to rescue, I became blocked."

That character had to take her own time to get through without being rescued.

"I had learned that lesson 15 years before as a pastor during a conflict that I was trying to step into. God had said then, 'I'll step in,' and that I didn't have to rescue everyone."

She also discovered spiritual lessons in trusting God's direction and God's plan. Comparing herself to others is fruitless. "We've been assigned a field where we labor; we get in trouble when we compare our work to others," said Brown.

She has seen God's plan at work throughout the Sensible Shoes journey. The first book was featured on the *Today* show thanks to interest from Kathy Lee Gifford. Brown has seen readers grow and change; seen her spiritual life become deeper and wider; seen God lead her to a career change wherein she writes, speaks, and leads retreats.

It's all about attentiveness, another spiritual lesson she gleaned.

"If we can practice attentiveness and notice what might be unusual and investigate that, that's when God reveals himself," said Brown. "The glory is that we really live differently in the world, we live sacramentally."

Brown admits to struggling with a loud inner critic, something many writers fight against as well. For Brown, it's another part of her spiritual journey.

"I had to learn to let Jesus shush her. This book is meant to be the offering of my best possible gift; if that is true, then I can let Jesus quiet the voices that tell me my gift isn't good enough."

••• Visit sensibleshoesclub.com •••

## Assignments

1.  List the areas where you struggle most with control. Your characters? Others' reactions to your writing? The publishing process? Be honest and thorough.

2.  How have you seen God's direction in your writing life? Where have you preempted God's direction for your own? Record your feelings about each instance.

3.  Describe several ways you can be more attentive to God. Also, describe the ways Satan keeps you from attentiveness to God's voice.

4.  What do your inner voices say about your writing? Create a conversation between Jesus and your inner voices, imagining what they might say to each other.

5.  How do you compare your writing—and publishing success—to others? List the ways that comparison hurts you.

# Writing Through:
## Traveling the Road of Resistance

## 7

ALISON HODGSON

"We're all pathetic resisters."

So says Alison Hodgson, author of *The Pug List: A Ridiculous Little Dog, a Family Who Lost Everything, and How They All Found Their Way Home*. She should know. She resisted writing every way possible and for some excellent reasons, including an arsonist burning her house down and a serious car accident while on vacation.

"After the fire I felt washed up," she said. "I prayed and surrendered everything. I knew that writing is part of who I am but didn't know what to do next."

The next day she received an email from an editor at houzz.com who, after reading her blog, asked her to write the fire story for the popular home/garden website.

She resisted, of course, because writing about the fire was hard. But she did it anyway, taking the next step through a door God had opened just a crack.

Hodgson is an old pro at resistance. She had begun blogging in 2005, quickly figuring out that a blank page was daunting unless she had a story to tell. She joined a writers group and attended the biennial Calvin College Festival of Faith & Writing in 2006.

"This was the first time I'd allowed myself to go to Calvin because I was all about the rules. I withheld that from myself because I wasn't calling myself a writer," she said. "But by that time I had been blogging for a year, so I felt I could call myself a writer."

Her takeaway from the festival? Blogging was less-than, that she should instead write a book. She quit blogging and refocused on a book, which meant she also had to write a proposal.

"I realize now the importance of small commitments," she said. "I had made a small commitment to write every day and post three to five times a week. At the festival, the best thing would have been to find places to submit essays or short articles to gain publishing credits."

Her decision to quit blogging stole her joy. "I felt like working on a book was real writing and blogging wasn't. I should have kept blogging and waited to see what emerged," she said. "I had been doing the work I needed to do, but I shifted and made it about something I wasn't ready to do. I ascribed to the convention of the time that blogs weren't that important. That something I loved wasn't worthy or enough."

The next five years were spent trying to write one book based on the fire and a second book based on her family's old cat. It didn't work, especially because of a terrible car accident, but it led to what became *The Pug List*.

"If I hadn't been asked to write the cat book, I don't know that I would have known to write the pug book. That pug was literally at my feet sneezing and breathing heavily," she said. "All those delays and distractions led me to write the perfect book for me."

She's had a few revelations and gained a boatload of experience along the way, especially when it comes to resistance.

First, perfectionism is a key form of resistance. Writers think their work has to be perfect the first time. It doesn't and won't be.

Second, press through the resistance to write or to work on a specific project. But if you truly get stuck, go back and figure out why. What is your resistance really about, and does it need to be addressed by other means?

Third, realize like Hodgson did that you're probably somewhere in the middle of the great swath of published writers. You're better than some, not as good as others. But that's okay. You can work toward improvement.

Fourth, realize that resistance takes many forms. Physical pain is one. Hodgson got a headache every third Wednesday of the month—the night her writers group met. After months and months of these headaches, she realized it was psychosomatic. She dedicated herself to going to the meetings, and the headaches stopped.

She also created her own set of rules about writing. While rules seem like a good idea—I have to write 500 words a day to be called a writer or I'm only a writer if I'm published—they are often about resistance to actually doing the work.

Fear is a huge form of resistance. Fear of failure, fear of success, fear of rejection, fear of writing the truth.

"I was afraid that if I became successful, I might not be able to handle the demands of that success and the demands of being a good mother," she said.

Fifth, resistance is a continual cycle. Just when you get through one wall, another arises.

"There are always going to be external and internal things that pull you off course, things than don't happen as planned," she said. "It's continually coming back to your commitment to write and to God's direction, provision, and grace. And keeping doing the work."

Hodgson is working on another writing project now and continues to write for houzz.com. Her family adopted a second pug; she's got young adult children and one in high school.

"We can't focus on the outcome; focus on moving forward, continuing to work and continuing to grow," she said. "We get so narrow about the opportunities to grow because they don't seem to be what we need or want. But take those opportunities when they come up. Keep knocking on doors and when there's a crack, step through it."

••• Visit alisonhodgson.net •••

## Assignments

1. What does resistance look like in your life? Create a list of the things that stop you from writing, including things like keeping a perfect house, continually meeting the needs of others, job, children, and parents.

2. Think about your fears. What are you afraid of specifically related to your writing? Write down those fears. Compare your resistance and your fears and see where they overlap.

3. Join a group of writers and spend time talking about the ways you resist. Not just good ol' procrastination, but the deep-seated resistance you feel as a writer. How many have similar forms of resistance? How many are different? How can you encourage one another through resistance?

4. Think about the ways you've overcome resistance, including even the smallest victory. Record those little wins. Meditate on that list, then write 300 words about how you've overcome resistance to keep writing.

5. What forms has resistance taken in your life, such as physical ailments or emotional struggles? What things that stop you from writing—even seemingly good things—might be your own resistance?

## The "No Pro": Facing Down the Inevitable Nos in Your Writing Life

**8**

CYNTHIA BEACH

Cynthia Beach is an associate professor of English at Cornerstone University and what she calls a "no pro." While she's had many articles and short stories published over the years, she's also faced a lot of "nos," especially when it comes to her novels.

It's discouraging, disheartening, and even a bit embarrassing for a professor with a master's degree in journalism and a Master of Fine Arts degree to not have her novel published, but Beach has learned a few things about "nos" along the way.

### Remind yourself that there are many reasons why a piece is rejected.

Getting the "no" from an editor hurts. "I have to work hard to tell myself why a piece could be rejected," said Beach. "Rehearsing these reasons can help me avoid the 'I'm not a real writer' trap."

Editors may have just seen something similar, it's not to their taste, or they may just be in a bad mood. None of this has anything to do with how good the piece is.

### Wanting to be published is okay.

Famous children's writer and illustrator Shel Silverstein said in a 1975 interview with Publishers Weekly's Jean Mercier, "People would say they create only for themselves and don't care if they're published. . . . I hate to hear talk like that. If it's good, it's too good not to share. That's the way I feel about my work."

Oregon writer David Oates recounted to Beach his experience when a poem he loved couldn't find a home. He "settled," he thought, for the local newspaper. A few years later he met a woman who told him that poem helped her and how she saved it to reread.

"This profound notion soothed me. I recalled a similar experience when a colleague cut one of my essays from our campus paper and taped it on her wall—and how ashamed I was that it had been published in the school newspaper instead of a 'real' journal," said Beach. "But that piece had given her something. Perhaps it had been for her all along."

### Waiting can be part of the divine process.

Waiting can be part of God's plan for your life. "Waiting certainly has been a part of mine," said Beach. She remembers waiting what felt like five decades for her first horse; she remembers what felt like another five decades for the love of her life to arrive, whom she married at nearly age 30.

"Will I find the hint of a perfect plan again in my current waiting when one of my novels finds a publishing home? I kind of think I might," she said.

### Being hidden can be part of the divine process.

Beach was particularly despondent one year at the Breathe Christian Writers Conference, wondering if her novel would ever find a publishing home. Despite her best efforts, it wasn't selling. Then friend and novelist Sharon Garlough Brown, author of *Sensible Shoes* and its sequels (see chapter 6), sat down and talked quietly about the spiritual concept of "hiddenness."

"She explained that sometimes God hides us for a time, for his purposes," said Beach. "This notion differed from hiding myself or from withholding—or any way of avoiding my calling. The hiddenness was God's doing and sprang from his all-seeing love."

### There are healing paths for this particular hurt.

Creativity guru Julia Cameron suggests an exercise she calls Blasting the Blocks when we're feeling banged up, frustrated, or despondent over our writing. She challenges us to journal these prompts:

- List all the fears and angers you have in connection to this project.

- Dig deeper to uncover hidden fears or buried anger.

- What do you have to gain by not doing this project?

- Commit this: Dear God, I will take care of the quantity, if you take care of the quality.

Beach has worked through these steps herself and found healing and a soothing calm. She offers these five suggestions for surviving the writing nos.

### 1. Lament the pain; nurture yourself.

Self-care is important when it comes to lament. Acknowledge that you feel loss and sadness. Treat yourself to something you enjoy, whether it's dark chocolate, binge-watching your favorite TV show, or going for a long run/walk/hike.

### 2. Pray for affirmation.

"I asked God, 'What do you think? Do you want me to continue trying to get this novel published? Will you send me affirmations if you do?'" she said. "Strangely enough, people began saying some really nice things. A student told me how she can't wait to read my novel. Another told me he wanted to change majors and go into writing."

She also noticed things coming her way: real people who mirrored and allowed her to deepen her characters, people who had lived where her novel is set, and a leadership position that helped her better understand her character.

"I had been blind to these incredible gifts before my prayer. Why hadn't I seen them before? In a sense, praying for affirmation primed me to look more closely," said Beach.

### 3. Create new work—don't sink into the revising-only loop.

"Recently the Guild, my writing group, gave me the gimlet eye. They challenged me to move on to something new while my unpublished novel, *The Seduction of Pastor Goodman*, waited for a response," she said. "Move on, Cynthia, they urged. Energy filled me. Okay, I decided, I will. And I did."

### 4. Find a nurturing writing coach, partner, or group.

"Sometimes I think that I wouldn't still be writing if I wasn't part of the Guild. We meet once a month and email about everything in between. We witness each other's moments of glory and of despair and hold them both with tenderness," said Beach. "They speak love and truth to me, and soon I'm on my way."

### 5. Let go of the results.

Our plan isn't God's plan, and we can't control the publishing industry. We can control our response to it, our writing, and our learning process.

"Let go, and go write," said Beach.

••• Visit facebook.com/Cynthia-Beach •••

### Assignments

1. What nos have you faced in your writing life? How did you handle them? List the good and not-so-good ways you dealt with those nos.

2. How have you seen waiting become part of God's plan for your writing life and your life in general? What benefits have you seen in the waiting process?

3. What self-care do you offer yourself when you receive a no? If none, what might you do to nurture yourself?

4. How does your writing community help you handle the nos in your writing life? How can you help others face the nos in their writing lives?

5. Read one of Julia Cameron's books, including *The Artist's Way: A Spiritual Path to Higher Creativity; Walking in This World: The Practical Art of Creativity; The Right to Write: An Invitation and Initiation into the Writing Life*, making a list of the ways to live creatively and handle the nos.

# The Craft of Writing

# Doctor, Doctor:
# Restoring Your Manuscript to Good Health

## 9

ANDY SCHEER

Andy Scheer has been editing in one form or another for decades. He worked on the editing desk of a daily newspaper for a year; he worked for five years at a professional association journal, learning from a peer who had been a fact checker for *Sports Illustrated*.

After a year at Denver Seminary he landed a job at *Moody Monthly* magazine, where he stayed for 18 years, 12 as managing editor. Scheer then moved back to his native Colorado to work for Jerry Jenkins and the Christian Writers Guild from 2002–10 and 2012–14. In between and now again, he's a freelance editor.

"I've been teaching people at writers conferences and in rejection letter after rejection letter since about 1988," he said. "I've seen a lot of what works and what doesn't."

Scheer remembers the first feature piece he edited for *Moody Monthly*. He thought he'd done a pretty good job until he got it back from Jenkins, then publisher for the magazine and Moody Press.

"Turns out the lead was partway down on page two and the article ended a couple of graphs before I thought it did, and in between lots of other words were taken out," said Scheer. "I've been learning from Jerry on and off for more than 30 years. In a few rare cases, I couldn't change anything of his and he couldn't change anything of mine."

Scheer lists three top mistakes fiction and nonfiction writers make:

1. Completely failing the opening pages. "There's no connection to the reader, no connection to the topic, nothing there to make people want to read, let alone buy, the book," said Scheer. "It's the 'so what?' factor."

Fiction writers fail when they don't begin with an interesting character in a unique situation. Nonfiction writers fail when they don't scratch where readers itch or even talk about the itch.

"Failing in any way to engage the reader is the worst kind of mistake," he said. He describes a recent novel (unpublished!) in which the writer used the first sentence to hint at the characters, then the next 750 words for back story.

"The writer had no knowledge of how fiction works in part because of not knowing craft, and in part by assuming readers are so interested in the topic that they will wade through waist-deep prose," said Scheer.

2. Muddling the point of view. Fiction writers at all levels can lapse out of a single point of view (POV) and begin to describe what another character is thinking. "Having worked with Jerry, who is extremely focused on POV, I know you have to have one tight POV per scene," said Scheer. "If novelists want readers to engage closely with the story, they need to be really careful with POV. This is one of the areas where novelists shoot themselves in the foot."

3. Wearing your own clothes. This means being yourself in your writing, talking eyeball to eyeball with your readers. Scheer admits to being heavily influenced by Les Stobbe, who has been in the publishing business for nearly 60 years.

"One of his biggest concerns is identification of the author with the reader," said Scheer, "coming alongside the reader and walking with them through the journey of discovery."

Scheer urges writers to be themselves, to not put on airs, to speak relationally.

Scheer is also a stickler for punctuation and grammar, but says those are the last things a writer should worry about. "Make sure the content is in place, that you are providing appropriate information to particular people in a way that communicates to those folks," he said.

Scheer often leads a workshop called "Big-Picture Editing" at writers conferences. He recommends assessing five areas to make sure your manuscript isn't doomed at the start.

1. Topic—Identify the topic in one sentence; if you can't, perhaps your goal isn't clear or you're trying to cover too much.

2. Theme—Identify the deeper, universal topic of your book and make it shine in your proposal and cover letter.

3. Audience—Picture one reader, not thousands, and write directly to that person.

4. Purpose—What does a reader take away from reading this book or article? Answer that, then include content essential to that purpose.

5. Angle—Decide the best way to present your material to reach your readers: personal narrative, allegory, how-to, humor.

Once you've considered these five areas, you are ready for a good edit by a competent editor. "If you can't cut 10 percent out of a piece without breaking a sweat, you don't belong in the business. There are precious few writers who know their craft so well that they don't need editing," he said.

Scheer recommends several good resources for those looking to hone their writing skills:

Brandilyn Collins has posted excellent material on the Christian Writers Guild blog and written the great book *Getting into Character: Seven Secrets a Novelist Can Learn from Actors*. Visit her website at brandilyncollins.com for more information.

- Roger Palm's book *Effective Magazine Writing: Let Your Words Reach the World*

- James Scott Bell's books *Plot and Structure: Techniques and Exercises for Crafting a Plot that Grips Readers from Start to Finish*; *Write Your Novel from the Middle: A New Approach for Plotters, Pantsers and Everyone in Between*; and many other books. Visit jamesscottbell.com.

- *The Elements of Style* by Strunk and White. Said Scheer, "Once you've got your audience, content, and message in place, and it's time to be concerned about language, a couple readings of this book will do the trick."

His best advice comes from the theme song of the vintage television show "Mister Ed": "People yak-it-ti-yak a streak and waste your time of day, but Mister Ed will never speak, unless he has something to say."

··· Visit andyscheer.com ···

## Assignments

1. Look at the opening pages of your book or the opening paragraphs of your article. Do they draw readers in? If you write fiction, do you drop an interesting character in an interesting situation? If nonfiction, have you identified and scratched the itch? Describe each.

2. Assess your book in light of who you are. Who are you when you write? Are you wearing your own clothes? Why or why not?

3. Consider your project in light of these five areas: Topic, Theme, Audience, Purpose, Angle. Write a sentence describing each one.

4. Look up Brandilyn Collins's and Jerry Jenkins's blog posts and read five each. Take notes on how their knowledge applies to your work.

5. Carefully read one chapter of your manuscript. Cut 15 words from each page. Now cut 10 more.

# Building a Book:
# Taking Writers Back to the Beginning

**10**

## MICK SILVA

Mick Silva, a cheerful and charming person, occasionally calls himself Dr. Evil Book Editor. That's because his job as a book doctor has him bringing his writer clients back to the beginning to get them started—or restarted—on the path to a great book and, maybe, publication. It's no easy task sometimes.

"I back writers up to their first vision, that first summary of what their book is about," said Silva. "Sometimes it takes weeks."

He asks questions: What makes your book unique? Why would anyone read it? What are its distinctives? Who is the audience? What is the felt need your book meets?

"I like to ask, 'If you don't write this book, how will your life personally be at stake?' I need that deeper reason because if you don't care enough to figure it out, then neither do I," said this former editor at several publishing houses.

Readers need something more than you, the author, feeling validated or fulfilled for having gone on the writing journey.

"What are you offering your reader that is fresh and new?" said Silva.

The first step in his book-doctor triage is getting back to the baseline reason for writing the book; the second step is creating a chapter-by-chapter map of the book. This is typically broken down into three acts. Act I is the setup; Act 2 is the complication; Act 3 is the resolution.

Between each act, he says, are major pivotal points. The first point forces you out of your normal. What changed? What event happened to rock your world? What force did you come up against? The second pivotal point, roughly between Acts 2 and 3, is discovering what God wants you to do after that life-altering event. How do you change? What changes in your life?

This prescription works for novels and memoir, his specialties. He loves life stories and personal experience tales.

"I also think of it as a roller-coaster ride. There's the big buildup—the slow ride to the top—then the exciting ride, then coming back to the beginning," Silva said. "There is the inciting incident, the fun and engaging adventure, then a return to the start."

He's found that writers are often intimidated by the title and role of "book doctor" until he explains that if your book is sick—just like your body—it needs to be fixed. He works on 10 to 14 books every quarter, all at different stages in the process. For $300 a month, each author gets a weekly phone call to talk about the book and up to 40 pages of editing during the month. Some coaching lasts more than a year; coaching for a novel of 350 pages lasts about 10 months. He'll also do intense editing (more than the 40 pages) for $3 to $4 per page.

"I come at a book from a reader's perspective; I look for where it's choppy, where it doesn't make sense. I also begin to see patterns related to word choice or pet phrases, or patterns of thought," said Silva. "I think like the universal reader to help diagnose where a book goes wrong."

He sees several common errors in the work of beginning writers. First is ignoring the age-old adage "Show, don't tell."

"Most writers describe what their experience was to make sense of the journey, but readers want to feel your emotions," said Silva. "I have to educate writers that readers want the emotions of the journey, not the lesson you learned. Writers think it's their job to teach readers, but our job is to lead readers so they can learn themselves."

Another common error is lack of understanding of basic parts of speech. He has to teach beginning writers the skills of compelling writing such as using active, not passive, verbs; strong, descriptive nouns; similes and metaphors; active and passive voice.

"Descriptive language that evokes emotion is mandatory," said Silva.

A final error beginning writers often make is not understanding that readers *want* to say, "Me too. You've put into words what I've been thinking." Silva likes to focus writers on their personal, particular journey and how that affected their lives; this honesty and openness leads to readers entering the story and making it their own.

"There are hidden lessons the book wants to teach, so I counsel writers to let go," said Silva. "Let go of teaching the lessons they've learned; open their hands to let the lessons go. Instead, show me you failed and how God showed grace to you."

Authors who do this well include Anne Lamott, Mary Karr, Nadia Bolz-Weber, Walter Wangerin, Rachel Held Evans, and Anne Voskamp.

Silva has several excellent pieces of advice for writers gleaned from years of working with writers at all levels of experience and by being a writer and reader himself (he admits to dabbling a bit in fiction).

**For beginning writers:** "Train yourself to write every day. Sit with your writing daily, show up every day. Writing takes a lot of time; it just takes time to write a great book."

**For experienced writers:** "Lots of writers get stuck in a creative cul-de-sac, get pigeonholed. Step out; be willing to risk in order to grow. So many don't see themselves as they could be and are instead just plodding along. Get creative. Don't hide your light, which God has given you to share."

••• Visit micksilva.com •••

## Assignments

1.  Write, in one sentence, what you think your book is about. Now spend a few minutes parsing that statement to discover the deeper reasons you are writing your book. Ask others for help if you need to.

2.  Think about the three-act book scenario. Outline your three acts in detail.

3.  Go back to your one-sentence overview. Now write a paragraph overview.

4.  What are your biggest struggles as a writer? Writing every day? Lack of grammar skills? Telling, not showing? Too much teaching? Are you pigeonholed? Write out a list of your struggles—and be honest. Ask others if you need to.

5.  Now list ways you can start to remedy those struggles. Remedies might include attending a conference; hiring a book doctor; reading good memoir; investing in a good writing tutorial; creating an official writing space in your home. Pick one you can start today and do it!

# Sell the Sizzle!
# How to Pitch Your Book, Article, and You

## 11

LORILEE CRAKER

Lorilee Craker helped write a book by a woman who had gone to prison and wanted to talk about how a marriage can survive a prison term. As Craker read through the original book proposal, she discovered a statistic on page 5 that said 95 to 100 percent of marriages fail if the spouse is in prison.

"That was the money statistic," she said. "I put it right at the top of the proposal."

She also put at the top of the proposal that this book was the Christian *Orange Is the New Black*, the popular and award-winning Netflix original show that chronicles the trials of Piper Chapman, a woman jailed for 15 months for a decade-old crime.

Craker is hoping her pitching expertise nets a book contract for the author, whose tale of embezzlement, prison, constancy, and love is sure to interest readers. Craker is an author who has honed her pitching skills on nearly a dozen books of her own, the most recent being *Anne of Green Gables, My Daughter and Me: What My Favorite Book Taught Me about Grace, Belonging, and the Orphan in Us All*.

"The overarching rule of all pitching comes from the old adage, 'Sell the sizzle, not the steak,'" she said. "What sets your story apart? What's the most marketable piece? The most distinctive? What does your project have that no other one does? That's the sizzle."

One of the problems, she said, is that authors are uncomfortable pitching their projects. They feel like they're hawking something nobody wants. "But authors need to change their mindsets," she said. "Know that the editor or agent wants to say yes. They need clients and need books to sell."

Craker sees four key places for an author to pitch a project: query letter, book proposal, one-sheet, and during a one-on-one meeting.

### Quick definitions:

Query letter—An email (usually) to an editor or agent introducing yourself and your project; three to four paragraphs long.

Book proposal—A document detailing your book project that includes overview, synopsis, bio, complementary titles, features and benefits, marketing plan, and sample chapters. See chapter 42 for in-depth details.

One-sheet—One page, including graphic elements, that introduces you and your project.

One-on-one meeting—Most often takes places during scheduled times at a writers conference; usually last 15 minutes.

"People think they need to be very businesslike when writing a book proposal or pitching, but it's sexier than that," said Craker. "There is more humanity to it because you're saying, 'This is what is so exciting about my story. I'm going to throw it to you and see what happens.' The pitch should be people relating to each other."

Craker urges writers to be specific in their pitches. A writer who says that his or her book is about the "Christian walk" isn't anywhere near specific enough. And perhaps doesn't know what the book is about. Narrowing the focus is key to any good pitch.

There are several key components to any pitch, whether a one-sheet, query letter, face-to-face, or book proposal. You can mix and match the ingredients in whatever pitch you're perfecting at the moment.

1. The hook or tagline. This is short, just a few words; a sentence that gets to the nugget of the project. Craker recommends studying movie ads for good examples of spicy taglines.

2. The what-if question. Craker created this question in the pitch for her most recent book: "What if a writer obsessed with all things *Anne of Green Gables* reentered her favorite story and discovered that it delighted her still and paralleled her own orphan journey and that of her daughter's?" It takes work to create a question, but a question begs an answer that publishing folks *want* to answer.

3. The logline—a one-sentence summary of the central conflict of the story. This is straight, factual and a hook for editors to hang their hats on.

4. A paragraph of action that describes the book and the reason for it, what sparked it, some event in the book.

5. Another paragraph of backstory with more details, particularly what led up to what happened to prompt the book or article.

6. The climax that brings it all together in a grand finale. Asks and answers what the reader will learn or take away.

7. Credentials of the author in one short paragraph.

"I do this in book proposals and queries to magazines. It's my basic formula for a good pitch," said Craker.

She uses several resources when planning her pitches. Look at lots and lots of book jacket copy, Craker suggests. What makes it good? What makes it interesting? Learn from its structure and word choice.

Also look at marketing copy for books that have done well, especially those similar to yours. Copy and paste into your file, then mimic its structure (not the words, of course). "I've found this to be super effective. Writing good marketing copy is an underrated skill," she said.

Comparison is also a good thing. Compare yourself in your pitch to other writers with similar tone and topic, but be realistic. Don't compare yourself to iconic authors such as Harper Lee or Shakespeare or Pierre Salinger, but do give editors something to hang their hats on.

She also urges careful attention to your book's audience. Know where you're aiming, or as her bookseller dad Abe Reimer used to say, "If you aim at nothing, that's what you'll hit."

"When you think of your reader, think of their perfect day. Know that audience so you can tell the agent or editor exactly who it is and be as specific as possible," said Craker.

Authors can hurt their chances for acceptance when they bury the lead, hide the sizzle while playing it straight, and hide unique things about the book or author such as a big blog following or tie-in to current news.

Craker knows that authors can be fearful about pitching a book to an agent or editor, or are worried about pitching that great magazine article idea.

"Don't park your personality at the curb. People want to seem professional and polished, but don't hide you," she said. "Be the you-iest you you can be."

••• Visit lorileecraker.com •••

## Assignments

1. Think hard about your book or article. Write down your short tagline and one-sentence logline.

2. Create the great what-if question for your project that will draw editors/agents in.

3. Who is the exact audience for your book? What kind of people are they? What might they do in a day? Describe your perfect reader.

4. What is the sizzle in your project? Really think through what you're selling and describe the sizzle.

5. Create the pieces described here, then mix and match to put together the start of a one-sheet, book proposal, query letter, and one-on-one pitch.

# Crossing Genres: Blending Fiction and Nonfiction Writing

**12**

CYNTHIA RUCHTI

Cynthia Ruchti wears many hats. She writes award-winning novels and nonfiction books that challenge and encourage. She writes for CBA's *Christian MARKET* magazine, and is the media relations coordinator for American Christian Fiction Writers (ACFW). She's also a literary agent with Books & Such Literary Management. How do all these roles create one writing career?

"Everything I write really falls under one umbrella. My brand is Hemmed in Hope," said Ruchti. "Because my brand is coloring all I do, it's not a drastic leap from novel to nonfiction."

For Ruchti, it's about passion. "When we're passionate about our roles and jobs, we don't have to create excitement for our writing. For me, I'm offering something—hope—that people already want so my passion comes out naturally in my writing."

Her first novel, *They Almost Always Come Home*, came out in 2010. Her first nonfiction was with a group of other writers and released in 2011 (*His Grace is Sufficient, DeCaf Is Not*). She is now working on her twenty-first book.

"The best kind of nonfiction keeps us engaged with story," she said. "The nonfiction I write are the books I'd like to hand to my fictional characters."

Ruchti credits her life experience with helping build a career that easily blends both types of writing. She started out working in a chemistry lab before leaving that job to be a wife and mother. But her brain craved something beyond the normal challenges of motherhood. She began taking correspondence courses through the Christian Writers Institute where she learned to write magazine articles, devotionals, and radio scripts.

That last assignment turned into a long-running gig writing slice-of-life vignettes for a radio devotional program that lasted decades.

"I got really good at stripped-down, evocative dialogue; I began wondering if I could write longer stories," said Ruchti. "This was certainly a good setup for writing fiction."

She began going to conferences to learn how to write fiction, joining ACFW in 2002. "I really felt like I had come home to where storytelling was common, where listening to characters in my head was normal," she said.

Enter those books that used her storytelling skills born of writing radio scripts and that came of age in both genres. The skills from one overlap with skills from the other and point to how a career set in both worlds is possible.

### The following skills cross from fiction to nonfiction:

1. Set the child in a reader's lap. Ruchti says that stats, stories, and videos are good ways to get a point across in a nonfiction piece, but "setting a child in a reader's lap" is the best way. Get nonfiction readers as involved in the story as fiction readers get in a novel.

   "Say I want to persuade you to give to a ministry in Africa. I can give you statistics about suffering children or show you a video, or I can bring you a starving child and lay him in your lap. Your soul responds if you hold that child, and that's what I'm trying to do with nonfiction," she said.

2. Write for multidimensional readers. Nonfiction readers are just as multidimensional as fictional characters, so hone your skills for creating complex fictional characters and then translate that into writing for readers that are equally complex.

   "Coming to understand that fictional characters are layered helps me understand that readers of my nonfiction are layered too," said Ruchti. "If I'm writing an article for parents, I need to have in mind that they are multidimensional."

### Several skills translate from nonfiction to fiction.

1. Make sure facts are accurate. A nonfiction writer must check facts, and a fiction author must do the same. A novel set in a real-life town must have the river flowing in the right direction, the streets named correctly, and the buildings placed accurately. Novelists can learn much from the fact-checking requirements of nonfiction writing.

2. Use good interview techniques. Nonfiction writers must know how to ask the right questions in the right way to get good answers; fiction writers can use those same techniques to interview their characters to get at the reasons they act a certain way. For example, the wrong question to ask a villain is "Why are you so mean?" The right questions are, "What is your wound? What circumstances brought you here?"

Some writers may have heard that readers of an author's nonfiction may not cross over to read that author's fiction, and vice versa. Ruchti found that there was more crossover than she thought. "I think it's because my books are aligned with my message of hope," she said. "The methods of using real concerns of the human heart can be expressed in fiction and nonfiction. Some readers may say that a certain book doesn't interest them but another one does, or a friend doesn't read fiction but my nonfiction may be of interest."

••• Visit cynthiaruchti.com and hemmedinhope.com •••

## Assignments

1. Spend time discerning the underlying theme of your writing. Ask yourself what your writing tends to focus on (e.g., guidance, hope, helping the vulnerable, sharing the love of Jesus, Spirit-led living). Ask friends, family, or fellow writers what they see as your theme. Write down your theme in a prominent place.

2. Describe the nonfiction and fiction you'd like to write or have written. How do these ideas or pieces reflect your theme? How might you rewrite them to reflect that theme?

3. If you write fiction, interview your characters to learn what motivates them, their deepest fears, how they were raised, what brings them the greatest joy.

4. If you write nonfiction, how can you add fiction techniques to your work? Where can you "put the child in your readers' laps"?

5. How might you expand your writing to include fiction or nonfiction? Consider newspaper articles, flash fiction, profiles, novellas, or blog posts.

# Stylin' It Big: Discerning Your Writing Style

13

JOYCE K. ELLIS

Eighteenth-century essayist Philip Dormer Stanhope, Earl of Chesterfield, distilled *style* this way: "Style is the dress of thoughts."

In general, I believe that *what we say* is content. *How we say it* is style.

Specifically, in the writing world, we use the word *style* in two different ways—writing to *fit in* (accepted style) and writing *to be you* (personal style).

## 1. Accepted Style

Accepted style is that which is acceptable and expected in the use of the English language, so as not to be thought of as a hick from Rubesville who don't know nuthin' 'bout puttin' sentences t'gither. Used this way, style includes such things as grammar, punctuation, capitalization, and proper word usage. It's a matter of learning the rules of the English language.

This is the "fitting in" kind of style. Learning these rules increases your likelihood of getting published (if the content is also there) because editors love to see manuscripts that don't need much work. Some star-quality writers break the rules at times. But as teachers often say, you have to know the rules in order to know when you can break them.

Each periodical and publishing house chooses a recognized style manual to be its standard (see sidebar). When editors make changes to our manuscripts, they aren't sadistically hacking up your slaved-over prose to get their day dose of jollies. Editors follow the rules of their designated style manuals.

In addition, they also develop what's called "house style," which codifies decisions they have made that either aren't addressed elsewhere or differ from the standard. Editors follow style-manual guidelines to smooth out our prose and help us communicate more effectively.

## 2. Personal Style

Personal style is your natural way of expressing yourself. Sometimes we talk about someone having a breezy style or contemplative style, a humorous style or ponderous style—or many others. Some writers' styles inspire a genre, like the hard-boiled style of a Raymond Chandler novel. Here are examples of various styles I have labeled these ways:

- Breezy:

  "He was a professional thief. His name stirred fear as the desert wind stirs tumbleweeds. . . . His weapon was his reputation. His ammunition was intimidation. . . . His presence was enough to paralyze" (Max Lucado, *The Applause of Heaven* [Thomas Nelson, 1996]).

- Much different but still breezy, maybe even quirky:

  "I walk along defending myself to people, or exchanging repartee with them, or rationalizing my behavior . . . or pretending I'm on their TV talk show or whatever. I speed or run an aging yellow light or don't come to a full stop, and one nanosecond later am explaining to imaginary cops exactly why I had to do what I did, or insisting that I did not in fact do it" (Anne Lamott, *Bird by Bird* [Anchor, 1994]).

- Contemplative:

  "If we let ourselves be paralyzed by fear we will not experience the mountain view, nor the thrill of finding our way into a wide meadow full of sunlight . . . or even the newly increased sensitivity of our ears and nose that comes when our eyes have been temporarily deprived of clear vision. Our risking in faith and obedience brings joy to our Master's heart" (Luci Shaw, *The Crime of Living Cautiously* [InterVarsity, 2005]).

- Humorous:

  "I cringed with guilt, imagining this saint who has worn out countless pairs of pantyhose at the knee, praying for lost causes and hopeless cases. . . . I feel puny and pathetic, for you see, I'm not a prayer warrior at all. I'm a prayer wimp.

  "Problems like the water heater exploding don't send a prayer warrior running from the house, in her ratty pink bathrobe and fuzzy purple slippers, screaming, 'Help, Lord! Save us!' No, a warrior never loses her cool like that.

"'Thank you, Lord, for this opportunity to wash the basement floor,' she intones" (Mary Pierce, *Confessions of a Prayer Wimp* [Zondervan, 2005]).

• Ponderous:

"In after days, when because of the triumph of Morgoth, Elves and Men became estranged, as he most wished, those of the Elven-race that lived still in Middle-earth waned and faded, and Men usurped the sunlight" (J. R. R. Tolkien and Christopher Tolkien, *The Silmarillion* [Del Ray, 2002]).

These examples demonstrate that personal style includes word choice, sentence and paragraph length, sentence complexity, density of expression, and more. It's the "feel" of the piece, how it flows, how much effort it takes the reader to understand it, how clearly it communicates, and how much it entertains.

## Varied Styles and Hybrids

We don't need to confine ourselves to a finite list of style categories. If you start pulling books off your shelf, trying to describe the author's style in a single word, you may get frustrated. We find many hybrids. Some authors write primarily in a simple and direct style with a dash of satire. We might classify others as mixing a conversational style with dry wit.

Styles, in general, have changed over the years too. Charles Dickens, for example, may not have found a publisher if he had lived in today's publishing climate—or he may have faced heavy editing.

And because various magazines have differing styles, you may also need to vary yours to fit in. But you shouldn't need to sell your soul over doing so. In other words, you might have to spiff up your outfit but not change your personality.

Accepted style and personal style are not mutually exclusive. The more we write and learn what's acceptable, the more we'll start seeing a blossoming of our own personal style that communicates well with the reader.

## Developing Your Style

Our own style develops as we read and write. It's like osmosis in plants. Everything we read soaks into our being and subtly shapes our style. We never try to mimic another person's style, but our personal style may reflect some of what we read. And the more we write, the more our natural personal style will emerge. Though we adapt slightly to fit in here or there, our writing personality will still shine through.

Kathrine Anne Porter, the Pulitzer Prize–winning author of *Ship of Fools*, encapsulated style this way: "Aristotle said it first as far as I know. . . . It is one of those unarguable truths. You do not create a style, you work and develop yourself; your style is an emanation from your own being" (*Writers at Work*, George Plimpton, ed. [Penguin, 1963]).

It's fun to write and then see how others describe your style. Quit worrying about it, and be you.

---

Joyce K. Ellis, "Stylin': What Is Style?" in *Write with Excellence 201: A Lighthearted Guide to the Serious Matter of Writing Well—for Christian Authors, Editors, and Students* (Grand Rapids: Credo House Publishers, 2017), 197-201.

••• Visit joycekellis.com •••

---

## Style Manuals – Joyce K. Ellis

Here is a list of the most commonly used style manuals, noting who uses them:

- *The Elements of Style, 4th ed.*, by William Strunk Jr. and E. B. White. Used by many writers in various areas of publication.

- *The Associated Press Stylebook (AP)*, by Associated Press (updated yearly). Used primarily by newspaper and some magazine editors.

- *The Chicago Manual of Style, Seventeenth Edition (CMoS 17)*, by the University of Chicago Press. Used by most book editors and many magazine editors.

- *The Christian Writer's Manual of Style, Fourth Edition (CWMS 4)*, edited by Robert Hudson, published by Zondervan. Based on principles of *The Chicago Manual of Style*, it delves deeper into specifics of style that Christian writers and editors encounter.

Writing style manuals are dictated by discipline, such as Modern Language Association (MLA) for English and the humanities, and the American Psychological Association (APA) for psychology, among others.

---

### Assignments

1. How would you describe your style? List a few words describing what you think your style is.

2. Ask several people who know your writing to describe your style. Does what they say match how you describe it? Why or why not?

3. Skim through some of your favorite books, making note of the authors' styles. List what draws you to each one (e.g., short sentences, flowery language, deep metaphors, clear and concise writing). How does your writing compare?

4. If you haven't already, purchase one of the style manuals listed above. Spend an hour or so perusing it to see how the guide works, what it offers, and how you can use it. Begin referring to it when you have style questions.

5. Study books, magazines, newspapers, and websites to see the differences in style between them. How will you have to adapt your style to difference writing venues?

# Exploring the Depths of Nonfiction

# Starting Small:
# Opening the Door with Devotionals

**14**

SUSAN KING

Writers eager to earn bylines, learn a new skill and touch hearts around the world will find a ready market in devotional writing. Publishers are in constant need of new material to fill print and online devotional slots and generally are open to working with new writers.

Susan King is executive editor of *The Upper Room*, a devotional started in 1935 that is 100 percent freelance written. She is always searching for 250-word, Bible-based devotionals to fill the pages of the popular little magazine that reaches around the globe.

"The Upper Room is the gold standard because editors know how exacting the requirements are," she said. "When editors see you've been published here, it tells them you can edit yourself and write tight."

The Upper Room receives 5,000–6,000 submissions each year for the 365 slots, which is roughly 920 submissions for each two-month booklet. A first-tier editor boils that number down to 125, then a second go-round boils it down again to 75–80, then to the final 61.

"For beginning writers, The Upper Room is wide open because it is all freelance written. It's also a great spiritual discipline," said King. "You're doing what all Christians should be doing anyway: connecting with God through Scripture. Why not write up your experience, get it published and share it with millions?"

Writing devotionals is also a discipline needing a different skill set from other kinds of writing.

"In order to get all we require in those 250 words, you have to say a lot with a little, which is tremendously challenging," said King, who figures she has perfected more than 8,000 devotionals—365 each year for 22.5

years. "Our purpose is to teach. We love it when a devotional is inspiring, moving, or entertaining, but we never sacrifice the teaching."

There are three elements to each piece:

1. Personal experience. This can be a story based on your experience, from the Bible, or a scientific, cultural, or historical fact. It should be unique and interesting and must be completely true. Verification must be provided for historical facts, and King urges (and urges again) that the butterfly/chrysalis example is beyond overdone.

2. Direct connection with God. An insight, a nudge from God, an "aha" moment, a Bible verse to connect with what we know of God or Jesus. "A prayer or Scripture isn't enough; we want God to have the credit," said King.

3. Application to life. Get from experience to application with specifics, details, concrete tools. Spell out the connection.

"No abstracts," said King. "Writers can hide in those abstracts. Writers have to understand the connection to explain it to others. Envision the reader as a nonbeliever with whom you would never use jargon such as 'the propitiation of sin.' Writers walk a tightrope between being preachy, being clear and fuzzying it up."

The Upper Room is equal opportunity, said King. It's open to the newest writers and to the most experienced. No resume necessary because each piece is judged on its own merit. The youngest to be published? Age 12. The oldest writer was 103.

"It's not about what you've done before; we judge by what's in front of us," said King.

··· Visit submissions.upperroom.org ···

---

## Additional Markets

Additional markets open to unsolicited freelance submissions include:

- Christian Devotions at christiandevotions.us
- Keys for Kids at keysforkids.org
- Mustard Seed Ministries at devotionals.mustardseedministries.org

Look for other markets in *The Christian Writers Market Guide* (Christian Writers Institute, christianwritersinstitute.com).

## Assignments

1. Find a print or online copy of The Upper Room (or devotional of your choice) and read one month's worth, noting the pattern of the meditations, kinds of opening stories, and how Scripture is used and applied. Take notes.

2. Describe in writing a recent "aha" moment you've had with God or a spiritual lesson that hit your heart. Now cut down that description to 75 words.

3. Record the direct connection with God, using Scripture, in 100 words.

4. Now write out the direct application of that lesson and Scripture in 75 words.

5. Prepare three devotionals and, following guidelines, submit at least one.

# Off the Beaten Path: Writing for Specialty Markets

## 15

LIN JOHNSON

Lin Johnson has written for specialty markets for years. She's boosted her clip file, her name recognition and her income doing devotionals, curriculum, study guides, and a host of other nontraditional writing projects. As director of the Write-to-Publish Conference, managing editor of *Christian Communicator*, conference teacher, and author of more than 70 books, Johnson is in a unique position to offer information and advice for those who want to break into specialty markets. She answers questions here.

**Please define "specialty markets."**

I use the term *specialty markets* to describe nonbook, nonarticle genres. These include curriculum, study guides, drama, devotionals, puzzles and activities, games, greeting cards, crafts, science experiments, and tracts.

**How might writing for such markets be a boost to a new writer's career?**

Since many writers are not thinking about these markets, editors receive fewer manuscripts, making sales easier. Some genres—such as puzzles, devotionals, and crafts—are easy entrees into publishing. Editors buying them often do not look for writers with writing credits. Thus new writers can boost their credits, which can lead to other sales and assignments.

**How might writing for these markets boost an established writer's career?**

These genres are faster to write than books and can bring in income between book contracts. Plus, with the decline of print magazines and a continuing emphasis on well-known names at many book houses, specialty markets provide other outlets for making money.

Proving yourself with a specialty markets editor can lead to steady assignments. For example, I've had curriculum editors give my name to other editors within their house and to editors at other houses, all who called me with assignments that kept me busy between books and helped pay the bills.

### What are some of the special markets available to writers?

#### Bible and school curriculum

Curricula are lesson plans and other resources to help a class or group study the Bible or other subjects.

Bible curriculum includes Sunday school for all ages with a teacher's manual, student book, sometimes a take-home paper, and a teaching aid packet w/visuals or DVDs; children's worship, youth group, club programs, vacation Bible school, reproducible books, Bible study / small group guides, and teacher training books.

Many church denominations, nondenominational houses, ministries, and homeschool organizations publish curriculum.

#### Bible study / small group guides

Although these guides fall under the curriculum umbrella, they are a separate category in the publishing world. Inductive Bible studies consist of questions to get people into Scripture passages to discover what God says and then apply those truths to daily living. They are not commentaries or lectures.

Most of them are designed to be used by small groups but can also be used by individuals. Others are designed only for individual use. These guides may be based on a Bible book or portion of a book, such as selected chapters from Isaiah, or a topic such as servanthood.

#### Devotionals

Devotionals are brief articles that explain a nugget of scriptural truth and apply it to our daily lives, linking our hearts—not heads—to God. They are rarely more than 200 words, although entries in devotional books may run up to 500 words. The largest devotional markets are booklets such as *The Upper Room*, *The Quiet Hour*, and many others.

#### Drama

Drama is writing for the ear not the eye, writing to be said not read. This genre includes:

- short sketches that introduce sermons or Bible studies or promote a ministry during announcements;

- choral readings divided for different voices and combinations of voices;
- monologues;
- puppet scripts, which are dialogues said through puppets; and
- full-length plays.

A few publishers specialize in drama books; other book houses, magazines, and curriculum houses publish them too.

### Puzzles and Activities

This category includes a wide variety of manuscripts such as

- crossword puzzles;
- word-search puzzles;
- mazes;
- connect-the-dots;
- secret codes;
- find hidden pictures;
- matching pictures, drawing lines to the same ones; and
- rebus stories in which pictures are substituted for some words.

These manuscripts appear in children's magazines, Sunday school take-home papers, puzzle and activity books, and children's bulletins.

### Games

Games are another fun way to learn, review lessons, or spend time with other people. They may be classroom games like a trust fall, lesson reviews based on TV quiz programs, physical games played outdoors or in a gym, travel games, and card or board games.

Games appear in curricula, homeschool magazines and books, church resource books, children's magazines, and Christian education magazines.

### Crafts, experiments, recipes

This type of manuscript focuses on written instructions for making an item such as a puppet, banner, or yummy dessert, or conducting an experiment using water, ice, and steam to illustrate the Trinity.

You can sell these manuscripts to children's, craft, and education magazines, publishing houses that do craft or church-resource books, and Sunday school take-home papers. You can also incorporate them into curriculum projects.

### Greeting cards

Walk into bookstores, grocery stores, drug stores, and many gift stores, and you'll see aisles of greeting cards for all ages and occasions. Because cards use few words, the writer has to make every word count while communicating as though talking with one person.

### Tracts

A tract is generally a small, four-page pamphlet that presents the plan of salvation in a creative way or encourages spiritual growth. Because Christians hand tracts to people, leave them in places where people might pick them up, or put them in bills with checks, the felt-need title has to compel the recipient to open and read the tract.

This market is dominated by Good News Tracts / American Tract Society and Gospel Tract Society, but smaller companies and denominational houses also provide opportunities for publication.

## How does a writer break into such markets?

Like every other type of manuscript, it's important to study writers' guidelines and samples. Because few books exist on how to write for specialty markets, it's important to spend time studying samples. For instance, if you want to write Bible study guides, work through a variety of guides in different formats and from different publishers to get a feel for what works.

Some of these genres, such as Sunday school curriculum and many devotional booklets, are written on assignment. In that case, you'll need to write a letter of introduction with your qualifications for writing that genre, enclose a sample of published writing, and ask for an assignment.

## What is the pay like?

The pay varies widely by genre and market. Unless you're writing a book, which is contracted like other books with payment negotiated in the contract, most editors pay a flat fee. For example, the common payment for daily devotional booklets is $15–$25 per devotional; greeting cards range from $25–$300 per card; and activities and puzzles in Christian children's magazines pay from $5–$100.

In the curriculum field, an editor may assign an entire quarter—teacher's lesson-plan book, student book or take-home paper, and teaching packet—to one writer or assign each of two or three units to different writers. Editors may assign some pieces of one lesson plan to different writers and pay by the piece. I've earned $150 for one case study and $4,000 for a quarter of curriculum.

Tract editors don't pay for these manuscripts.

## What resources can a writer use to learn more about these markets?

If you live near a Christian bookstore, especially a large one, browse for examples and talk with the manager or owner about potential markets.

Few books are in print on specialty markets. Check in writing books that have chapters on writing different kinds of manuscripts, but you won't find chapters on all the markets I have identified.

*The Christian Writers Market Guide* (Christian Writers Institute, updated annually) has sections on devotionals and greeting cards, as well as topical listings for devotionals, puzzles, and other categories.

---

## Specialty Market Resources

While few specific resources exist for writers wanting to tap into specialty markets, several tried and true books, listed below, offer valuable knowledge and background. All are available new or used on Amazon.

**Curriculum**—Most of these books are written for teachers but give writers necessary background to write lesson plans.

- *Christian Education: Foundations for the Future*, edited by Robert E. Clark, Lin Johnson, and Allyn K. Sloat.
- *Creative Bible Teaching*, by Lawrence O. Richards and Gary Bredfelt.
- *Design for Teaching and Training: A Self-Study Guide to Lesson Planning*, by LeRoy Ford.
- *How to Ask Great Questions*, by Karen Lee-Thorp (also good for Bible study / small group guides).
- *Learning Styles*, by Marlene D. LeFever.
- *Living by the Book: The Art and Science of Reading the Bible* (book and workbook), by Howard G. Hendricks and William D. Hendricks (also good for Bible study / small group guides).

**Bible Study / Small Group Guides**—Valuable for writers.

- *How to Lead a LifeGuide Bible Study*, by Jack Kuhatschek and Cindy Bunch.

**Drama**

- *Playwriting: A Study in Choices and Challenges*, by Paul McCusker.
- *Scriptwriting: Building a Writing Ministry for the Church & Beyond*, by Martha Bolton and Kimberly Messer.

**Other Resources**

- *1001 Illustrations that Connect: Compelling Stories, Stats, and News Items for Preaching, Teaching, and Writing*, by Craig Brian Larson and Phyllis Ten Elshof.
- *Complete Guide to Bible Journaling: Creative Techniques to Express Your Faith*, by Joanne Fink and Regina Yoder.

## Which specialty markets seem to be the most open right now?

Daily devotional booklets are always open markets since content rarely is recycled. Magazine editors who publish specialty manuscripts like puzzles, crafts, and activities are actively looking for these.

## How have you written for these markets?

I've made most of my writing income from specialty markets. For almost four years, I wrote four curriculum books—along with student take-home papers and teaching packets—one per year. I've written dozens of other curriculum pieces, ranging from a unit of study to a case study for one lesson, and for all ages, although my specialty is junior high through adults.

I've also written a dozen Bible study guides (all but two of them on assignment), hundreds of devotionals, and everything else except greeting cards as parts of lesson plans.

I discovered early in my writing career that one of the advantages of writing for specialty markets is getting to know editors who offer a steady stream of assignments, if they like your work.

## What is your best advice for writers trying to break into specialty markets?

Read and use a variety of samples. Spend at least a couple of hours reading samples of the type of writing you want to try. Use Bible study guides from different publishers for your own quiet time. Make a few crafts published in a magazine or book, and work a few puzzles. Volunteer to be part of a drama ministry at your church.

Once you have a grasp of how to write these types of manuscripts, do your marketing homework like you would for articles and books. Then start sending queries and submitting manuscripts. You may find your writing specialty in specialty markets.

••• Visit writetopublish.com •••

## Assignments

1. Consider the specialty markets listed and decide which might be appropriate for you.

2. Begin gathering information on specific markets, including publishers/editors, writer's guidelines and samples. Use *The Christian Writers Market Guide* and publisher websites. Make a folder for each and keep all information in one place.

3. Study three to five examples from the genre in which you're interested, such as greeting cards, dramas, or curriculum. What did you like about those samples? Dislike? What would you do differently?

4. Pick one example and try writing in that genre. Consider where you have experience—skits, curriculum, puzzles—and concentrate on that. Put together three or four samples.

5. Using the guidelines and contact names you've gathered, write an email of introduction and include samples, if required. Send off three queries.

# Content Is King: Article Writing for Magazines, Websites, and More

## 16

ANN BYLE

Writing articles for magazines, newspapers, websites, newsletters, and a myriad other outlets is a great way to start and maintain a writing career. Those outlets need content, content, content. Writers are poised to provide it.

A writing career can seem daunting for those just starting out. Writers must build contacts, write great stories, find reliable sources, meet deadlines, and keep editors interested with new ideas and new takes on evergreen topics. Even established writers can hit dry spells, or be affected by disappearing markets, burnout, or new editors who don't know them.

Fortunately, the need for content remains king, and those who can write a top quality, well-researched article will always find work. Here is a list of tasks a writer must accomplish to get articles published regularly.

## 1. Understand the query letter or email.

A query letter or email is you, the writer, asking the acquisitions editor if he or she is interested in your idea and/or article. Be as specific as possible, citing your topic, sources, and why you are qualified to write this piece for that specific magazine. Your qualifications can include that you're an expert in the field, have other articles to your credit, or have great sources. Be respectful, professional, and offer no editorializing such as, "I'm the most qualified person on the planet to write this piece."

TIP: Several things to include in a query: article title, brief synopsis, list of sources you'll use, brief bio, proposed length, and when you can have the article ready. Keep it to one page.

TIP: Almost all editors accept email queries. Check writer's guidelines to be sure.

### 2. Find the right editor.

Finding the right editor's name can be like mining for gold: difficult and time-consuming but, ultimately, a huge payoff. For magazines and newspapers, study the masthead located somewhere in the first couple of pages. Also take advantage of the publication's website, which often includes a section titled Writer's Guidelines. Other resources include the annual *Writer's Market* (Writers Digest Books, released annually) and *The Christian Writers Market Guide* (Christian Writers Institute, released annually). You can also use Internet search engines to query, for example, "Acquisitions Editor, Oprah Magazine."

Address your query to a specific editor in a specific department, if that information is available.

TIP: Don't address a query "To Whom It May Concern." Be as specific as possible, for instance: Acquisitions Editor, Women's Issues, Children's Department. Use a name if at all possible and spell the name correctly.

### 3. Find good sources.

You've been assigned a story on fly-fishing, about which you know nothing, for a local magazine. A simple Internet search reveals a fly-fishing store just a mile from your home, so you head over for a visit. There you meet the owner or an employee and you talk to the two customers who come in while you're there. You've got your sources.

Another example: You want to write an article about postpartum depression because your sister experienced it. You can read other articles on the topic and contact the sources cited there; do an Internet search for postpartum depression experts; contact your own OB/GYN. You'll want several expert sources and at least one story about a mom who has experienced this.

If you are writing for a national publication, include sources from a variety of places around the country. If writing for a local publication, use local sources.

TIP: Tap into the people you know, ask your friends on social media for ideas about who to contact, use the Internet to search for experts. There are websites out there dedicated to linking sources with article writers.

### 4. Get the word count right.

Editors ask for a word count for a reason, so keep close to what they request. Ten to 20 words short or long isn't usually a problem; even 50 words can be acceptable. Occasionally, however, you'll fall way short. See where you can deepen and lengthen by doing another expert interview, adding another anecdote, or researching another angle.

You can also add a sidebar, especially if your story is complete but has some interesting related topics. Sidebars can include lists, Q&As, and tourist information.

Going over the count is fairly common for writers. Delete redundancies.

Synopsize some of the quotes or explanations. Cut out material that doesn't fit the article's focus. Then tighten your sentences and paragraphs by deleting extra words. If you are really stuck, ask a writer you trust to help you cut words.

If you must, ask the editor about lengthening the piece. That editor may say yes, but be ready to cut when he or she says no.

TIP: Don't request word count changes the first time you write for an editor. Do what they ask the first couple of times; only after you've established a relationship can you ask for more space.

TIP: Use the material you deleted from the piece for another article. Also, know that most writers use only a portion of the information they have gathered.

### 5. Focus your article.

If you are unclear what your assigned article is about, first go back and look at the notes (or emails) the editor sent. If you are still having trouble, ask the editor for clarification. For example, an editor asks you to write a piece on an upcoming concert and gives you 500 words. After a little research, you discover several aspects of the concert that are worth mentioning.

Asking the editor will help you narrow the piece to writing about the musicians, focusing on the charitable cause the concert benefits, or about the controversy surrounding the venue. The editor may even assign you another story!

TIP: Write a one-sentence thesis statement that summarizes the article. Once you have that focus, you can tailor interviews and research to that thesis.

### 6. Don't bury the lead (or lede).

Most articles put the best stuff at the top, then fill in the picture with additional information. To discover the best lead, ask yourself these questions:

What is the timeliest information to share with readers? (A popular singer is coming to town for a concert; a fund-raising picnic raised $20,000.)

What is the most important information to share? (A well-known ministry leader is retiring; a new church building is the first to be LEED certified in the city.)

What is the most unique information to share? (A novelist wrote about cell memory because she has a friend who experienced it; a best-selling author struggles with the same topic she writes about.)

TIP: An editor may decide that he or she wants a different lead. Don't panic. Editing is as much about opinion as about good grammar and sentence structure. Her opinion isn't wrong; it's just different from yours.

### 7. Offer a unique take on a usual topic.

Editors are always going to run articles on prayer or weight loss or parenting techniques or the holidays, but they always want something new.

You can provide them with that new twist by using a little imagination. Let your mind wander, let your fingers do some Internet research, or let your eyes look at everyday things in a new way. You'll be surprised at what you come up with. Here are some examples:

For a piece on holiday gift-wrapping, focus on using baskets instead of boxes for your gifts.

For a piece on summer activities for children, highlight several easy science experiments instead of museums/sandboxes/play dates.

For a piece on prayer, talk about walking a labyrinth as a prayer starter instead of creating a prayer journal or gratitude list.

TIP: Whether your article is assigned or you are searching for a home for it, use a little imagination to add sparkle and uniqueness.

### 8. Become an expert in your field.

Consider where you are already an expert. Do you homeschool your four children? You're an expert in homeschooling techniques and curriculum. Do you love to knit elaborate sweaters? You're an expert in yarn choice and knitting techniques. Do you love to hunt with a crossbow? Are you a lawyer? Electrician? High school English teacher? You're an expert in those fields already. Write from your experience.

Also, begin writing about a topic and do several articles. Go back to that story on fly-fishing. You learn a little about it for the article, even try fly-fishing on a local river. Now you know enough about it to query an editor on one aspect of fly-fishing, such as tying flies or choosing the right rod and reel. A second article appears on the topic, and suddenly you become an expert. No, you don't know everything about fly-fishing, but you know who to ask, what to ask, and where to sell your stories.

TIP: Don't sell yourself as an expert in fields where extensive education is needed. You can't be an expert on Christology if you haven't been to seminary; you can't be an expert on surgery techniques if you aren't a surgeon. Editors are looking for credentials in the field about which you write. They will be justifiably nervous about publishing a piece in a journal for seminary professors by a person who says, "I've read about the book of Revelation for years and feel like I've got my own interpretation of this section of Scripture."

TIP: You can write an article about such topics if you plan to interview sources that know about surgery techniques or End Times prophecy. Tell the editor whom you plan to interview.

### 9. Keep good records.

Freelancers need to keep track of what they have submitted, where, run dates, deadlines, payments, clips, and much more. Software abounds, so choose what works best for you even if it's notebooks and pens.

Keep track of every published article, whether print or online. Get a copy of print articles (usually a publication provides this), print out online articles, or keep a file of online links to your pieces. You will be surprised how often you refer to these clips, either to list in a resume or query or to use at speaking engagements.

A nice clip file revives your spirits when you get down about your writing career. You can look at what you've written and where it's been published, and feel just a little bit better.

TIP: Set aside a drawer in your office file cabinet or create a separate computer file for URL links. If the hard copies get cumbersome, begin keeping just the article, not the whole publication; be sure that those articles include the publication name and date.

TIP: Things to keep track of—contact names and emails/phone numbers; clips; payments; deadlines; submissions; mileage; business-related meals, hotel, travel costs; conference fees; office expenses; educational fees; professional magazines.

### 10.  Sit down and get started.

Probably the hardest thing about your freelance career is getting started. Take small steps first, moving on to bigger and bigger steps until you see your first article in print.

Small steps: Get a good desktop or laptop computer; create a writing space; purchase or borrow the *Writer's Market* or *The Christian Writers Market Guide*; visit your local bookstore and peruse magazines for article ideas or possible publication places; make a list of article ideas.

Larger steps: Search out writers' guidelines for publications you'd like to write for; write a query email; interview several sources; write the actual article.

Biggest steps: Send a query email to an editor; send off that article to the publication of your choice; begin a second, third, and fourth article.

TIP: The biggest and best thing you can do to become a go-to writer for online or print publications is to actually sit down and write. Like Maria and Captain von Trapp sang, "Nothing comes from nothing; nothing ever could." Begin today.

••• Visit annbylewriter.com •••

## Assignments

1.  Make a list of topics you can or would like to write about for magazines or websites. Divide topics into areas of expertise and areas of interest. Enter the list either in Excel or another format.

2.  Research magazines and other outlets (via market guides or websites) as markets for the articles you'd like to write. Add the publication name/URL to your chart next to the appropriate article. Also add word count requirements, editor's name and email.

3. Choose one topic and begin outlining the article. List the points to cover, experts to interview, and possible leads. Research as necessary, including finding/contacting the experts.

4. Gather all the pieces to your article—interview notes, research results, anecdotes—and begin writing, keeping to the word count specified in the information about the publication.

5. Put together a query letter/email, following the guidelines above. Before sending, proofread carefully and/or have a writing friend proofread for you. Once it's perfect, push "send."

# Writing Well with Others: Collaborative Writing and Ghostwriting 17

GINGER KOLBABA

Ginger Kolbaba has written books with survivors of 9/11, adoptive moms, business leaders, and celebrities. She has started from scratch with some of her subjects, come into the middle of a flagging project, and stepped in to fix a manuscript that wasn't publishable.

Kolbaba has seen it all when it comes to cowriting and ghostwriting, and has much advice about this rewarding opportunity and revenue stream.

First, start with articles. Start writing as-told-to pieces or other stories to learn the craft and begin to understand what a larger project will entail. Shorter pieces allow you to discern which scenes to include, which details to leave out.

"Books are really hard to do, so people want to know what you have done," said Kolbaba. "If you have a portfolio that shows you can write well and work with people, it's a good sign. Showing up at a writers conference and asking an editor to assign you a book isn't going to work."

Second, cowriters have to be able to capture the subject's voice. "You have to know it's their work, not yours," said Kolbaba. "That person may not talk like you or have the same mindset, but you have to set that aside to capture his or her voice."

Kolbaba records every interview to help her reproduce her subject's voice as well as to keep facts straight.

Another requirement is good writing skills. Collaborative writers have to know grammar, the best themes to undergird the story as well as themes that won't work, and which stories fit into a manuscript.

"Some stories are powerful but don't fit into the book," she said. "But it's a great story to use in a blog post, a magazine article, or in another book.

Writers have to hone their skills to know what to put in, what to leave out, and how to use diplomacy to help figure that out."

A fourth requirement for good cowriters or ghostwriters is the ability to get information from people when they don't want to give it to you or don't think it's important.

"I once wrote a book for a woman whose son was a famous athlete, but she didn't want to tell their whole story," said Kolbaba. "She wanted to gloss over the important parts that readers would want. It took a lot of trying, as kindly as possible, to get that information."

Collaborative writing takes a certain kind of personality. If you have a short temper, are very opinionated, have to control everything, or just don't work well with others, collaborative writing isn't for you. There is too much negotiating involved, too much knowing when to step back and when to barge ahead.

Kolbaba does as much research as possible on her subject before interviews begin, which allows her to focus on the details. "I don't want to ask a question I already know the answer to," she said. "I ask them what something looked like or smelled like, which often brings out other good information."

Kolbaba has developed several interview tricks over the years. She tries not to ask yes/no questions, instead asking questions that lead the subject to disclose more details and deeper information. She has learned how to lead her subjects back from verbal rabbit trails, gently returning them to the subject at hand with leading questions.

She also has learned to sense when her subject needs to take a break. "If I sense they are getting tense or bored, I ask about photos or move to another line of questioning," said Kolbaba.

She often asks subjects about their earliest memories. "This throws them, but gets them thinking and begins to create a sense of trust," said Kolbaba. "Nine times out of ten those memories won't be in the book, but they build a sense of trust."

And trust is the key component when it comes to co- or ghostwriting. The subject needs to trust you, the writer. "They need to trust that you'll love their baby as much as they do," said Kolbaba. "Your job gives you permission to be super nosy and dig to get the best details and information."

So what about payment? What about taking on jobs you're not excited about?

Kolbaba has indeed taken jobs for the money. One job had her miserable from start to finish, but it also taught her to trust her gut. "Sure, I got the money; but what I gave away in exchange—energy, time, happiness—wasn't worth the money," she said.

Be careful doing work for friends or friends of friends. Writing a friend's grandmother's story can build your resume, but writing that story can be like lending money to a relative. Tensions can arise and feelings can be hurt.

Kolbaba urges writers to not work for free. Some subjects want a writer to do the work for free, promising to pay when the book gets published. No, she said. "A writer can't work without getting paid, and can't be responsible for what the subject needs to do to make that happen," said Kolbaba.

There are some people Kolbaba just isn't comfortable working with, something all cowriters will face. Personality differences and subject matter are two reasons that cowriting or ghostwriting may not work.

"When I'm not comfortable working with someone, I say that I'm not the right person and suggest others," she said. "And if I'm not interested or excited about a project, I'll ask a lot more for payment. It's something you'll have to figure out and navigate."

••• Visit gingerkolbaba.com •••

## The Three Big Questions – Susy Flory

Susy Flory is coauthor of the New York Times best-seller *Thunder Dog: The True Story of a Blind Man, His Guide Dog, and the Triumph of Trust* (by Michael Hingson) as well as other books. Her career as a cowriter has taught her to ask three questions before embarking on a book project:

1. Why are you writing this book?
2. What is your message?
3. Who is your target reader?

She recommends that coauthors or ghostwriters look for clients who are teachable, are open to the book growing and evolving, who are willing to go to the hard places, and who trust you as a writer.

Flory offers this advice for those interesting in collaborative writing.

1. Educate yourself on the industry to get a sense of what topics are commercially viable and which aren't, and whether traditional or self-publishing is the best option.
2. Understand book marketing and PR to help the client; most won't understand it.
3. Work well with others. Sometimes you'll have to be bossy, and other times you can follow them where they want to go.
4. Keep your ego under control.
5. Earn your credentials on smaller projects.
6. Have a business sense for contracts.
7. Make sure your name is on the cover.
8. Read Cecil Murphey's book *Ghostwriting: The Murphey Method*.

••• Visit susyflory.com •••

## Assignments

1. Rate yourself on a scale of 1 to 10 on these traits: perfectionism, control, temper, bossiness, gentleness, kindness, patience, self-control. Now ask someone else to rate you. If you're high on the first four, you might reconsider your dream to be a collaborative writer.

2. Start small by doing an as-told-to piece for a magazine or website. Make a list of subjects, then match with publications. Choose one and contact the person.

3. Practice asking leading questions by asking a family member these questions: What is your favorite dinner and why? Why do you like the color yellow? Where do you want to be in five years? Who is your best role model? When have you felt happiest in your life?

4. Research blogs, magazines, and books about the cowriting or ghostwriting process. Once you're done, reassess whether you're ready and willing to move forward.

5. Read several books that have been cowritten to learn more about how to keep the author's voice and let them tell his or her own story.

# An Editor Speaks: Writing for Women with Depth and Authenticity

**18**

## JUDY DUNAGAN

Judy Dunagan has a heart for women that beats back to her days as a pastor's daughter, through her years teaching women's Bible studies, and into her time on the women's ministry leadership team and later staff at Woodman Valley Chapel in Colorado.

So it wasn't a stretch when she accepted the position as acquisitions editor for Moody Publishing's women's line, a job she's held since August 2014. It didn't hurt that she also helped her dad, Mark Bubeck, refresh his best sellers *The Adversary* and *Overcoming the Adversary*.

"My deepest heart is discipleship and helping the Word come alive for women," said Dunagan, who lives in Colorado Springs. "Moody was looking for someone who had a heart for the target audience, discipleship, and good writing, and also a heart for millennials."

Those millennials are reading books with depth, not fluffy shallowness. Young moms love practical books on being a good mom, as indicated by the popular blogs they're reading, indicated Dunagan. Authentic intimacy is really resonating.

"Women are talking about the subjects they aren't getting in church or are going to the Internet for answers," she said. "Women want studies about who we are in Christ, stories of hope in the storms of life because life is hard. It's important that Scripture comes alive and women can practically apply it to their daily lives."

Dunagan is constantly searching for authors who can resonate with women. She attends writers conferences, speaker training events such as Advanced Writers and Speakers Association (AWSA) and Speak Up, and reads blogs to see who is saying what.

"I look for authors for whom writing is a calling and a passion," she said. "These women not only have a love for writing, but are doing it for God. If I sense that an author is about being famous or seeing her name on a book, I don't want that."

Platform is important, but it's not the end-all for Dunagan. "I want to discover someone with a true heart, not necessarily a huge following," she said.

Dunagan also knows what she's looking for regarding topic. While much has been done about the different life stages a woman faces, including a number of books for single moms, she's seeing a shift. "For awhile it was all about us because women felt they couldn't tell their stories in church, but now the Lord is shifting it to be more about him, who he is, and praise and worship. These kinds of books are selling now."

Themes include making Scripture come alive, helping women know Jesus more, and making disciples who can make more disciples. "It's always about going back to him. The Holy Spirit is really moving, and authors are going deeper. Writers talk about their journeys, but it's about how God has used that journey, how he has built compassion in the author, how God meets people," she said.

Dunagan's search for authors of deep books for women means she's come across some duds. One of her biggest pet peeves is cutesy titles, particularly those with food in the title. She also doesn't like feeling talked down to in a book, too much of the author's story and too much salacious detail.

"These are desperate times and women want books that can help them," she said. "I have a pretty open heart, but when an author keeps telling me how many books she's written I'm not sensing a lot of humility. I love to see an author with a sense of calling, a sense that the Holy Spirit is doing something."

She sees many books presented to her before they're ready. Writers should learn how to study God's Word and teach it. She encourages authors to get a writing coach, attend conferences to see how the business works, interact with other writers, and start building a platform. That platform might be blogging, speaking, or starting a ministry.

"But a lot of women aren't teaching because they think they have to be like the speakers they see on videos," said Dunagan. "I'm encouraged when women are beginning to be out speaking."

She's excited that Moody is publishing Bible studies for women. "Women are hungering for the Word and for more than just fluffy studies," said Dunagan. "I want writers who have a passion to write and who write through their insecurities because if a message changes the writer it can change the readers."

••• Visit moodypublisherswomen.com •••

## Assignments

1. Think about the last three Bible studies you did, either on your own or with a group. What did you like about each one and what did you dislike? Did you feel talked down to? Were they too easy or too hard? Make a list of what you like in a women's Bible study.

2. Have several readers go through your Bible study and make a list of what they like and where they stumbled. Find people who are honest and who have done Bible studies through the years.

3. Consider teaching a Bible study to gain experience and to work through your materials. If teaching scares you, teach to yourself at home and mark where you need to deepen, expand, or cut back.

4. Research writers conferences in your area and sign up to attend one.

5. Begin praying daily for the women who will work through your Bible study, for God to work through you, and for God to reveal what your true message is to your readers.

# Writing Memoir: Reflecting on Sections of Life

## 19

ERIC L. MOTLEY

Memoir offers both readers and writers unique opportunities. Authors can share their deepest thoughts, spiritual struggles, and life lessons, while readers can relate to and learn from the struggles and growth of their favorite writers. Memoir can plumb the depths of one person's life the way no other genre can. Authors from Shauna Shanks and *A Fierce Love: One Woman's Courageous Journey to Save Her Marriage* to Nadia Bolz-Weber and *Accidental Saints: Finding God in All the Wrong People*; from Mary Karr and *Lit: A Memoir* to J. D. Vance and *Hillbilly Elegy: A Memoir of a Family and Culture in Crisis* are offering up their stories.

Eric L. Motley has also authored his debut memoir *Madison Park: A Place of Hope*. Motley's memoir focuses on place—the place that birthed him, raised him, and to which he returns in his heart every day. Motley was raised in Madison Park, a small town near Montgomery, Alabama, that was started by newly freed slaves. His grandparents raised him, as did all the church ladies, his grandfather's friends, all the neighbors, and his teachers.

"In the last five or six years there has been an enormous number of memoirs published, many by African-American men. I wanted to add my voice to that chorus line so that a different narrative can be appreciated," said Motley, an executive VP at The Aspen Institute, a think tank dedicated to addressing the world's biggest problems. Before coming to The Aspen Institute, he worked in government posts and was special assistant to President George W. Bush.

"This memoir is two stories: my story and the story of Madison Park, which are so intricately interwoven," said Motley.

Writing *Madison Park* wasn't just a walk down memory lane. Motley's experience no doubt mirrors that of other memoir writers who seek to tell the deep truths of their lives—and thus speak into the lives of their readers.

"The nature of memoir requires a type of honesty and forthrightness not easily achieved. When I decided to tell my story, there were a lot of emotional and psychological boxes that were sealed," he said. "It was hard retrieving those boxes, opening them, and acknowledging that this stuff

---

### Memoir vs. Autobiography – Cec Murphey

Cec Murphey, esteemed elder statesman of Christian publishing, wrote this blog post about the difference between memoir and autobiography.

For the past few years, I see *memoir* used incorrectly—even by publishers. A memoir refers to anecdotes or events in a person's life. A book of memoirs is a collection of such anecdotes.

"An autobiography recounts the author's entire life, usually from birth until the time of the writing. A memoir focuses on one aspect or period of the author's life.

For instance, if Hillary Rodham Clinton wrote a memoir, she might call it *A Million Miles* to refer to the 973,000 miles she traveled while she was Secretary of State. If she wrote her autobiography, she might call it *Being My Own Person*. This second, not-very-good title would be an examination of her entire life.

We write memoirs and autobiographies in first person, and they are an attempt to convey a true account of what happened. We expect both to give us personal information and let readers see into our thoughts and actions.

But the purposes of the two books differ. The memoir focuses on specific instances. *The White House Years* would be a good example. Memoirs usually cover a brief span of time, and their main purpose is to draw the reader's attention to a specific theme or circumstance.

Look at this title: *We Were Soldiers Once . . . and Young: Ia Drang—The Battle That Changed the War in Vietnam* [Presidio, 2004]. Harold G. Moore wrote this book about a particular period in history and his subtitle explains his purpose.

The book I wrote for Don Piper called *90 Minutes in Heaven: A True Story of Death & Life* [Revell, 2014 anniv. ed] has some biographical information, but the focus is on his death-and-return-to-life and his recuperation. That's properly a memoir.

However, I wrote the autobiography of Dr. Ben Carson called *Gifted Hands: The Ben Carson Story* [Zondervan, 1991]. The subtitle makes it clear that we tried to cover his entire life from his birth until we wrote the book. *Gifted Hands* came out in 1990 and has remained a good, steady seller. The 20 plus years since publication doesn't make it less an autobiography.

---

Cecil Murphey, "The Difference Between Memoirs and Autobiographies (Part 1 of 2 and Part 2 of 2)." Posted March 22 and March 26, 2013. http://cecmurpheyswritertowriter.blogspot.com/2013/03/

would have to be dealt with in this manuscript. It was not easy acknowl-edging that I had anger and disappointment in family members that I needed to deal with."

Motley got help from friends and readers who told him that parts of the story had not been fully told. He needed to dig deeper, open more boxes, and get to the why questions.

"Good writing causes you to acknowledge the why questions. Why did this happen? Why aren't you talking about this? Why are you emotionally removed from this?" he said.

Not that it was easy for Motley. His grandfather was stoic and even-tempered, given to saying little. "And we didn't reveal our personals out on the line," said Motley.

The book became a spiritual exercise, a recognition of the familiar and also about the strength he found along the way.

"Should the book never have been published, it was about my own journey, about rediscovering myself and those in my life, and dealing with unfinished business," he said.

Motley loves reading (and writing) poetry and memoir, would love to see his poetry published one day, and has a couple of screenplays in mind including one for *Madison Park*.

He understands the importance of memoir. "Memoir helps us see the poverty of our own situation and God's grace. We see our dependence on others and our dependence on something much larger than ourselves," he said. "Reading others' memoirs allows us to be more reflective about our own lives. We are all born the same and we all die the same. There is much to learn from each other."

••• Visit aspeninstitute.org •••

## Details about Memoir

- 55,000–75,000 words
- Biographical information included, but doesn't bury the focus of the book
- Stories point to the underlying theme
- Can be written at any time of life (autobiography tends to be written later in life)
- Leads readers to look at their own hearts and lives

## Assignments

1. Read three memoirs and record what you like and dislike about each one. What are the underlying themes for each memoir?

2. Think about themes in your own life and potential memoir, like forgiveness, second chances, redemption, place, a quest. Now find several stories from your life that exemplify those themes.

3. Does your book seem more like a memoir or an autobiography? What are the characteristics of each? Why will you choose one over the other?

4. List five reasons why people might be interested in your memoir. What makes your story unique, or what does it offer to readers?

5. Create a chapter-by-chapter outline for your memoir, listing the events you want to talk about and the life lessons you learned for each chapter.

# Discovering the Breadth of Fiction

# The Heart of a Poet:
# Writing to Challenge Readers

**20**

LORA HOMAN ZILL

Lora Homan Zill has four jobs. She teaches composition and critical analysis at Gannon University in Erie, Pennsylvania. She is artist in residence for the Pennsylvania Council on the Arts and its Erie Arts & Culture branch. She owns and publishes the poetry magazine *Time of Singing*. And she is a poet in her own right with more than 30 poems published and many more written.

*Time of Singing*, started by the American Baptists back in 1958, is published four times a year by Zill through her Wind & Water Press. Poets from all over the world contribute the 40–45 poems in each issue that range from free verse to haiku, sonnet to villanelle.

"I read at least 300 poems for each issue," said Zill. "If I see God/sod or moon/June, I reject it. If you talk about grace and mercy, which can be religious jargon, I send it back. I want to know what you mean by *grace* and *mercy*."

This reader of more than 1,000 submissions a year has seen it all: from exceptional to good, from bad to worse. One of the biggest reasons she says no to a submission is lack of awareness of the art and craft of poetry.

"Poetry is worthy of your time and devotion," she said. "I spend as much time on a poem as I do on a prose piece. It takes a long time to throw one pot or carve a duck decoy or quilt one square. Poetry takes just as long and just as much effort to learn to do well."

Another reason she says no is a poem's lack of anything fresh to say. "Poetry, like any art, is to wrestle with a question. A poem should pose the question and wrestle with it so I can too," said Zill. "Art gives you the space to wrestle with humanity, God, evil."

Preachiness is a third troublesome issue. Poems shouldn't be preachy; "poems are invitations to coffee, not a finger-paint sermon," she said.

Finally, poor craft. "Some writers have a poor understanding of the craft of poetry; it's not just the end rhyme, but internal rhyme and rhythm as well," Zill said. "But it's a craft you can learn and through which you can express yourself."

The best poetry, she said, offers an image, a riff on that image, and then lets the reader make his or her own inferences. "That's why I love poetry so much: the trust between the readers and the writer. If you don't have that, the poem doesn't work," she said.

Zill asks the big questions about art, creativity, and spirituality. "Why don't Christians see art as a spiritual experience?" she said. "We're suspicious about art because it's our imagination. We are well practiced in the negative aspects of imagination but not so good at the positive parts of imagination. We've lost that exploration of creativity and the imagination."

She is exploring the creative in several ways. She's making a stained-glass window for her church and working a book tentatively titled *Imagine: How to Satisfy Our Insatiable Longing to Feel God's Pleasure.*

"Jesus is the creative Word of God," said Zill. "Your artistic nature will lead you into more than one area. The creative impulse will compel you to explore other arts, which makes you a better artist in your chosen field."

She offers several pieces of advice for those who want to explore creativity and imagination through poetry.

First, read poetry. She recommends Christian poets Madeline L'Engle and Luci Shaw, but also encourages exploring Ted Kooser, Billy Collins, Jane Kenyon, and Denise Levertov. "Read them all; get an anthology," she

---

### Reading *Ghalib* – Robert Hudson

This is the trade I want:
to gather sheaves of jute and hemp
with broken hands
in a field flat with sun
to twist them into ragged strands
and loop them over nails
in a fly-thick shed that smells
of sweat and saffron paste
to braid them into rope
thick as some fat mullah's wrist

to soak them in a yellow brine
and fold them into knots
beautiful impossible coils
with the white horizon
of desire secretly bound inside
and when they have dried
hard and tight as river rocks
to sell them in the loud bazaars
so that anyone with a few rupees
might have the frantic hateful pleasure
of untying them again.

---

Robert Hudson is author of *The Christian Writer's Manual of Style, 4th Edition* and *Kiss the Earth When You Pray: The Father Zosima Poems.*

said. "You have to read poetry to get the idea. Ask yourself how much exposure to the language you have, how much poetry you read."

Second, grasp the strengths and weaknesses of words, sentences, rhythm, rhyme, meter, different kinds of poems, and other aspects of the craft of poetry. All that reading will help you with understanding language and how it works. Language is, after all, the tool of the craft and any expert knows his or her tools.

Third, practice. "Write a poem a day, even if it's four lines," said Zill. "If it's a priority, you'll do it. You have the time to eat, read, sleep, go to work. If you want to be a poet, you'll find time to write poetry. There are seasons of life for sure, but writing poetry will always come back to being a priority."

She is also quick to credit the necessity of an intuitive feel for poetry. "God gives people an intuitive feel for raising goldfish or woodworking or writing devotionals or whatever. That intuitive feel is needed for writing poetry and sometimes you just don't have it," Zill said.

Ask for advice, consider your gifting, and find out what others see in you. Discover what makes you glad and brings you pleasure; that's probably your gifting.

As for writing poetry, "A good poem will challenge our assumptions; all art should challenge our assumptions," said Zill. "Don't confirm my worldview; challenge my worldview."

••• Visit timeofsinging.com •••

## Assignments

1. Check out a poetry anthology from the library and read through it. Record which poems speak to you and why, and which poems annoy you and why. Read Robert Hudson's poem (see sidebar) and record how it speaks to you about the writing life.

2. Read through several of your poems and look for clichéd rhymes (God/sod, moon/June, tree/free) and Christian jargon. Rework those poems or start over altogether.

3. Set aside at least half an hour each day for a month to write poetry. Keep a record of how many poems you write and/or revise. At the end of the month, decide if you want to add another half hour each day.

4. Explore several poetry sites or magazines such as *Time of Singing*. What kinds of poems are featured? What are submission guidelines? Choose a poem to submit and do so.

5. Consider what other art forms might enhance your creativity. Research classes to learn skills in dance, stained glass, pottery, sewing, drawing or furniture refinishing. Try a couple of things and record how your creativity grows.

# Read, Write, Watch:
# Pumping Your Screenwriting Muscles

21

BILL MYERS

Ask Bill Myers for his best advice on building a screenwriting career and it boils down to three words: read, write, and watch. Read books on screenwriting. Write lots of screenplays. Watch lots of good and bad movies and figure out what makes them that way.

"Every movie has strengths and weaknesses," he said. "If you're studying film as a screenwriter, study those movies with great elements. Great elements are the scenes, characters, and structure that you can't forget."

Books on screenwriting are fine, he said, but they tend to be formulaic, and formula is what sells. "But if you want to be a great screenwriter, learn the rules and then figure out how to break them well," he said.

Myers also recommends writing a whole lot of screenplays, most of which won't get beyond your computer. He wrote really bad screenplays before he began writing better ones. Then even better ones, then good ones, and finally great ones. He's won awards for *McGee and Me!*, the television series he pioneered with Ken Johnson about an 11-year-old boy and his imaginary friend who use the Bible to help them navigate through growing up.

Myers has had nearly 130 books published and close to two dozen of his screenplays produced. He's written dozens more that may yet make it into production.

"The biggest mistake screenwriters make is not rewriting enough," he said. "Writers think the screenplay is done but it's really not. Generally, I think my first draft is brilliant, but I let it sit for a couple of weeks, then I say, 'Man, I'm glad I didn't send that out.'"

Myers is a man-of-many-talents who has spent a generation plying his trade. He teaches screenwriting, cofounded Amaris Media International, and is always writing and working toward producing quality products.

Current projects include producing the film *Eli*, based on his book of the same name that has sold 100,000 copies. He's also developing a series of children's movies based on his children's book series The Incredible Worlds of Wally McDoogle.

"It's uncharted territory trying to reach the general market with engaging stories that include an element of God without preaching and that make viewers walk away with a higher estimation of God," said Myers. "That's what we're trying to do with Amaris."

Myers has valuable counsel for writers looking to make it as a screenwriter.

1. Find the balance between derivative formula and out-of-the-box originality. "You want to land somewhere in between," he said. "You want to be commercial but you don't want to be formulaic."

2. Your dialogue has to dance, not just move the story. "Many writers see dialogue as a necessary evil instead of enjoying it as an art form," said Myers.

3. Develop depth in your characters. "Never go with your first idea for a character because that character is always a cliché," he said. "It'll always be derivative from what you've just seen. Think awhile about the characters."

4. Find the films (or television shows) that excel in a certain area and study them. Some films excel in character, others in concept or setting or dialogue.

Myers has been watching a lot of television because it's so good these days. Great writing and great series make it a great medium to study. "Television is a writer's medium; movies are a director's medium," said Myers. "If you are writing comedy, watch the comedies. If you're writing quirky stuff, watch reruns of *Arrested Development*. If you're looking for good structure and plot, watch the *Lie to Me* series. You can let your characters live and breathe when writing for television."

One of the age-old questions for writers is whether you write for yourself or write to the market. Myers's success has come from not writing to the market. All those screenplays he wrote that were rejected because of a faith element? He turned them into novels.

But he keeps writing screenplays and he keeps learning his craft. "You do your due diligence. If you're serious about your craft, you darn well need to write and practice. You keep falling down and you keep getting up," he said. "And you keep knocking on doors. Being good is no assurance that you'll succeed. Persistence is."

Myers admits to knowing a dozen writers who are better than him, but who will never get published or produced. Why? "Because hard work and persistence win the day; talent doesn't."

Streaming video, on-demand television and movies, Hulu and Netflix make for a great learning environment for screenwriters. There's benefit to binge watching, said Myers. Watching one episode after another lets you figure out what works and what doesn't.

"If you want to be a screenwriter, be a screenwriter," he said. "But it's not the road to fame and fortune. There are ways to be a successful screenwriter without writing for a big studio. You can make films for your church or with college kids. It's not about the big brass ring that so few get."

••• Visit billmyers.com •••

---

### Bill Myers's Favorites

Bill Myers's favorite films:

- Inception
- The Martian
- The Matrix (the first one)

Bill Myers's favorite screenwriting books:

- *The Hollywood Standard: The Complete and Authoritative Guide to Script Format and Style*, by Christopher Riley.
- *The Hero's Journey: A Voyage of Self Discovery*, by Stephen Gilligan and Robert Dilts.
- *The Screenwriter's Bible, 6th edition: A Complete Guide to Writing, Formatting and Selling Your Script*, by David Trottier.
- *Screenplay: The Foundations of Screenwriting*, by Syd Field.

---

## Assignments

1. List five of your favorite films and the reasons you like them. Now list five of your least favorite films and why you didn't like them. Compare the lists. What stands out?

2. Do the same with five television shows you like and five you don't.

3. If you don't own one of the screenwriting books listed, either order one or check one out from the library. Mark the pages that strike you as most important.

4. Reread a screenplay you've written, considering characters, dialogue, setting, and plot. What appears derivative? Original? What parts need work? Devote an hour each day to improving your screenplay.

5. Research places in your hometown (or a bigger town nearby) where you might take classes, attend seminars, or meet with others to talk about screenwriting.

# Short and Sweet: Writing Flash Fiction

## 22

BEN WOLF

Flash fiction is drawing speed-readers, best-selling novelists, and writers who have little time but lots of ideas. The genre of five-minute stories is growing as quickly as each one can be read.

Ben Wolf is one of the experts in the field. He is owner of Splickety Publishing Group, which publishes three flash fiction magazines: *Splickety*, *Havok*, and *Spark*. Each publishes ten to twelve flash fiction pieces per issue, and each has four issues per year.

Wolf defines flash fiction this way: a story of 1,000 words or less with a beginning, middle, and end that has character development, plot, setting, tension, and conflict.

"Every word counts," he says. "Any excess dialogue and description that can be done without should be done without. It's challenging, but it's also fun."

Splickety magazines have featured best-selling Christian authors such as Jerry Jenkins and Brandilyn Collins, though some authors have turned down requests to write flash fiction because they weren't sure they could do it.

"The authors who have taken a crack at it have enjoyed it and thought it was a really good exercise," said Wolf.

Why try this seemingly limiting genre? "Writing flash fiction teaches you to write tight," said Wolf. "It's a great way to learn how to wield the craft a little better, it's a pretty low commitment, and most can turn it around in a day or less."

He also points to the benefit of learning to fit everything important into a small package, which helps when you go back to your longer novel.

"Writing flash fiction helps you zero in on basic story structure and gives you the opportunity to hone all the elements of great storytelling in a small space. And you get a nice break from whatever big project you may be working on."

He has used flash fiction to get unstuck in his own writing. "If you're knee-deep in your novel and all jammed up, writing flash fiction can unlock what you need to go forward," said Wolf.

The biggest mistake: "The most common mistake we see is that people write about something that has already happened," said Wolf. "Flash fiction is about something happening now."

He offers two comparisons. Flash fiction is like taking a camera and filming a fire, not a news story about it later. It's about being in the car accident, not remembering being in a car accident.

"Start with something happening and make sure something keeps happening," he says. "This is not the time to sit and ruminate about the past. Flash fiction isn't sitting there explaining something or thinking about something."

Here's an example from a post on the Splickety blog titled "Santa Hood" by Emma Carrie: "Robin Hood peeked around a pine tree at the empty street. No princesses, ninjas, or teen turtles with bulging bags of candy. No parents with flashlights. Now his crew was the only costumed group here." (Carrie, Emma. "Santa Hood." Posted Oct. 16, 2017. *Splickety: Flash Fiction.* http://splickety.com/santa-hood-flash-fiction/)

The first publication was originally titled *Splickety Magazine* and it focused on general flash fiction. After Wolf took over the magazine from its original owners, he renamed it *Splickety Prime.* "We were getting lots of speculative fiction stories, but that wasn't the focus of the magazine," said Wolf. "A friend suggested different magazines."

*Splickety Prime* was renamed in 2014 (it started in 2012) and is now *Splickety. Havok,* which publishes sci-fi and fantasy flash fiction, and *Spark,* for romance flash fiction, began in 2014.

The Splickety publications aren't limited to Christian fiction; they publish a lot of general market fiction, but the company is mostly run by Christians who, at this point, are volunteers. Wolf points out that the Bible is full of flash fiction, from Jesus' parables to Old Testament stories such as the tale of left-handed Ehud stabbing the obese king of Moab and losing the knife in his fat rolls.

Wolf foresees flash fiction growing in popularity in the years to come. He'd love to create an app for users to receive daily flash fiction, and foresees a YA magazine in the Splickety portfolio.

"With the way technology is going, it seems natural that fiction would get shorter and have more punch," said Wolf. "It will have more impact and provide a powerful emotional experience in a shorter amount of time."

Wolf is always looking for more flash fiction, for which writers receive

$0.02 per word when accepted for publication. He recommends writing 700–750 word stories because the magazines publishes only two 1,000-word pieces per issue. Chances of publication triple with a shorter piece.

"We get plenty of decent stories. We always need more excellent ones," he said.

••• Visit splickety.com •••

## Assignments

1. Read through 1 and 2 Samuel and Judges and look for examples of flash fiction. Do the same with the Gospels and Acts in the New Testament. What do all these stories have in common?

2. Compile a list of action verbs and strong nouns that you could use in writing flash fiction.

3. Take one scene from your current work of fiction and create a 1,000-word piece with beginning, middle, and end, as well as character and plot development. Now cut it down to 750 words.

4. Check out *The Rose Metal Press Field Guide to Writing Flash Fiction: Tips from Editors, Teachers, and Writers in the Field* by Tara L. Masih (also look for a similar title for nonfiction flash writers). What advice from the book applies to you? What did you learn?

5. Research Splickety's formatting and submission guidelines and contest themes, then submit your flash fiction story.

# Deepening the Details: The Palette of a Research Artist

**23**

## TRACY GROOT

Tracy Groot has won three Christy Awards for her historical fiction. *Madman* is a fictionalized account of the Gerasene demoniac set in Jesus' day. *Flame of Resistance* is a tale of World War II spies and betrayal in France, and *Sentinels of Andersonville* an account of the infamous Civil War prison. Her novel *The Maggie Bright* is about the famous British rescue of its army at Dunkirk.

All different; all meticulously researched. All filled with tiny details that add depth and gleam and that only a dedicated and creative research expert could unearth.

Groot has thrown herself off a boat in the Mediterranean Sea to see what Jonah might have experienced. She talked with a WWII fighter pilot, walked former battlefields, wandered through small French towns, and boarded boats along an English quay.

"Research is a lot more creative than you would think," said Groot. "It's about being intuitive. Your intuition for tracking down a story will take you places you hadn't thought of before."

Groot is a firm believer in reading, reading, reading. The Internet, she said, is just a jumping-off point for discovering experts and their books on a given topic. Her home library includes Josephus, Winston Churchill, sailing books, books about Jewish culture, battle memoirs, and anything else that might be useful. Her best find, she said, was an excavation report on the town of Kursi, which gave her the name of the demoniac from whom Jesus cast multiple demons into a herd of pigs for her book *Madman*.

What started as interest in the topography of that area ended with a name: Kurdus. Her protagonist finally had a name thanks to one obscure book!

She admits that some of the books are mighty dry. "You have to be willing to pay the price, and the price is the time to read the book," said Groot. "But if I find a few good details, it's worth the time. Every book is some parts drudgery and some parts sheer creativity."

Groot also advocates site visits. She's been to Israel, Greece, Turkey, Cyprus, London, Dover, Dunkirk, Andersonville Prison, and Gettysburg. "Visits can connect you with actual people," she said. "That's what's fun: striking up a conversation with people at the places you visit. If they don't know the answer, they generally know someone who does."

For her novel *The Maggie Bright*, a walk along a quay looking at boats led to the discovery of a small boat with a plaque labeled LSD, which stands for Little Ship of Dunkirk. She'd found a boat that had saved soldiers' lives all those years ago. One conversation led to another and pretty soon she was on a yacht, also an LSD, exploring its deck while the owners entertained.

Groot takes meticulous notes on the books she reads and copious photos of the places she visits. Notes are filed by topic, as are maps, brochures, notes taken on movies and conversations, snippets of dialogue, descriptions of scenery, impressions, and Internet information. She also keeps a detailed bibliography.

"I work my way into the book by compiling thousands of notes and putting them in file folders. I read all that stuff and ideas start germinating. Once I do the final go-through for the book, I throw away descriptions and dialogue and bits like that, but keep any facts and figures. It's my way of backing out of the book," said Groot, who recently spent five days at a cottage organizing a decade's worth of research for a book based on the biblical Jonah story.

When she's writing, her office is filled with photos on poster board of the places she's visited. Details such as the way a rope lays on a deck or a certain smell or the way a bridge looks are brought to life by those pictures.

"Looking at pictures can evoke being in that place; they bring you right back," she said. "Photos also give you minute details you wouldn't have noticed."

Groot has taken advice from two well-known names in American and British history.

Tom Brokaw once said, "It's always a mistake not to go." That advice has indeed brought her around the world.

British historian Arnold Toynbee said this: "Character is formed by an interaction between a person's heredity and his response to his environment."

Those words have taken her deep into her characters' pasts and cultures, as well as into their environments, "putting where characters have been into where they are now" in her novels. "Where my characters come from has huge bearing on how they are going to respond to their environments now," she said.

Toynbee's words have also changed the way she looks at her work-in-progress, a book she started years ago and is going back to now. This time, she said, she'll look at her research differently and write differently.

"All the stuff that goes into research is joy to me. I'm excited to get started on another project," she said.

$$\cdots \text{ Visit tracygroot.com } \cdots$$

---

## Visual Inspiration

Tracy Groot suggests surrounding yourself with either memorabilia of the project you're working on or with pieces that inspire you, including books, photos, and even plastic figurines. Charles Dickens holds pride of place on her desk as inspiration.

She also has whales big and small and a Jonah figure on her desk, all to evoke her book about the runaway prophet.

"My first ten years of writing was on a buffet table stuffed into a hallway alcove. But when you habituate the space, you come to love it as you fill it with even small things like a candle or a figurine. It's all about immersion."

---

## Assignments

1. Think about the space where you write. Have you made it yours in some small way? If not, how might you do that? If so, look around and revel in the space you have.

2. Organize the research you have done (or will do) for your historical novel. You may need to purchase file folders or devise a system, but begin organizing now. What are you missing? Maps? Diagrams? Photographs? Begin gathering those things.

3. Plan an itinerary for a visit to the location of your novel. Where would you like to go? What season? What side trips might be in order?

4. If you can't visit your location, search out other resources such as documentaries or feature films about that area, YouTube videos, virtual tours, maps or brochures you can order, books to borrow or order online, or people who have visited that area. Take notes on what you find.

5. Think through how your characters' past culture and environment would impact them as they populate your novel. How can this understanding deepen your novel? Begin making changes now.

# The Long Road: Building a Novel and a Career

**24**

SARAH SUNDIN

Sarah Sundin has published ten novels, but her long road to publication and fiction success offers beginning novelists a road map to learn from and follow. She shares her peaks and valleys, as well as vital craft issues to master along the way.

**Peak 1:** God called her through a dream to be a novelist in January 2000.

"I woke up from a dream so compelling that I had to write it as a novel," said Sundin. "But I was a pharmacist, not a novelist. That dream became a novel that will never be published."

**Peak 2:** She met Kathy Collard Miller (kathycollardmiller.com) thanks to Sundin's mom bragging about her novelist daughter to her bowling team. Miller was on the other team and suggested Sundin buy and read *Christian Writers Market Guide* before giving her a call.

"I called Kathy in April 2000 and asked her all the newbie questions. She gave me two pieces of advice: join a writers group and go to a writers conference," said Sundin.

**Peak 3:** She found American Fiction Writers in Sacramento and attended the conference. She had one completed novel and was almost done with the second, "which I thought was a masterpiece."

She walked in and met Lin Johnson (see chapter 15) at the book table and asked which book she should buy to get her first novel published. Johnson recommended *Self-Editing for Fiction Writers* (see Assignments) but Sundin demurred, figuring she didn't need it because she'd done so well in English classes.

**Valley 1:** Sundin attended Lee Roddy's workshop at the conference, then bought *Self-Editing for Fiction Writers*. She cut her novel from 750 to

350 pages, joined a writers group in January 2001, and brought her edited masterpiece.

"I read the first chapter and they laughed in the right places, then praised me for dialogue and characters but said the story was iffy," remembers Sundin. "I went home and cried, and got back to work."

She worked and learned and worked more hours, juggling her role as wife and mother of three and her part-time work as a pharmacist. Sundin cut and rearranged and cut again.

"I learned my words were not Holy Writ, and if I wanted to be published, I had to do the work," she said.

Novels one and two were set aside when Sundin conceived a seven-book series of six contemporary and one historical novel. She decided to start with the historical about a World War II B-17 bomber pilot.

"My writers group was key because I kept learning. I would come home and cry, edit more and bring it back. This went on for two years," said Sundin. "I needed signs and they were there, but I was doubting all the way until finally in 2003 my writers group said it was time to get to Mount Hermon Christian Writers Conference and begin shopping the novel."

**Valley 2:** Sundin met with novelist Lauraine Snelling, who told her she was writing at a publishable level. Sundin then slogged through five years of rejections. By then she had two books in the (now) historical series done and the third outlined.

**Peak 4:** On Sept. 12, 2008, she got an email from Revell acquiring editor Vicki Crumpton saying they wanted the series. She screamed and wrung her hands until her husband finally brought the phone and told her to call Crumpton.

---

### Three Vital Aspects of Fiction Craft

Novelist Sarah Sundin says it's vital for novelists to master three aspects of fiction craft to create great novels.

1. Story structure. "Once I understood story structure and how plot works, I could take the story and make it fit the structure," she said. "When my agent said I had a slow beginning, I knew where to trim because I knew story structure."

2. Point-of-view. "Get fully in the character's head: seeing, hearing, feeling what they feel, seeing their world through their eyes," she said. "Everything should be written from a character's POV: their senses, vocabulary, history, and voice."

3. Personality types. "If you don't understand personality types—introvert/extrovert, thinker/feeler—you'll write all your characters like you," said Sundin. "Truly get into a character's skin."

Her first novel came out in March 2010, a decade after that original dream.

Sundin has great advice for writers who dream of publishing novels.

"Join a writers group, go to conferences, and keep writing," she said. "Don't get stuck on that first novel; start new projects and keep learning; and go to conferences to learn about the industry, meet people in it and have them get to know you."

••• Visit sarahsundin.com •••

## Assignments

1. Sarah Sundin recommends these books: *Getting into Character: Seven Secrets a Novelist Can Learn from Actors*, by Brandilyn Collins; *The Writer's Journey: Mythic Structure for Writers*, 3rd ed., by Christopher Vogler; and *Self-Editing for Fiction Writers: How to Edit Yourself into Print*, by Renni Browne and Dave King. Purchase or borrow all three to read and take notes.

2. How have you handled the peaks and valleys in your writing career? Do you have more valleys than peaks? Journal your thoughts on both.

3. Research conferences and writers groups in your area. Make an action plan on how to join a group and attend a conference.

4. Read articles, blogs, and books to learn about POV. What POV do you use in your novel? How many? Do you jump POVs? How can you fix those jumps?

5. Learn more about the many personality types out there. Which type are your characters? Are they all the same? Different? What is your personality type?

# Bringing the Past Alive:
# Characteristics of a Top Historical Novelist

**25**

JOCELYN GREEN

Jocelyn Green has published over a half dozen historical novels and novellas, each of them set in North America during the eighteenth or nineteenth centuries. *Wedded to War* was a Christy Award finalist and *The Mark of the King* won a Christy in the Historical Fiction category. Green, recounting her journey to historical fiction writer, remembers one historical novel she read that caused her to think hard about her own work. She didn't like that novel for two reasons:

1. It didn't anchor her in the story world. "It was like I was watching the characters move across a blank stage," she said. "My five senses were not engaged; it was not immersive."

2. The characters didn't react to the history happening to and around them. "In historical fiction, it's critical to have characters being proactive and interacting with the history going on around them," said Green.

Green's definition of a historical novel is this: "A historical novel tells a story that cannot possibly be told in any other setting or historical context."

That means you can't just plop a romance in 1865 and ignore the Civil War. Or toss a romance into Victorian England and ignore the courtship rituals of the time. Or set a story in World War II France and forget about the German occupation.

"The sense of history and the characters cannot be separated," said Green. "They interact with each other in critical ways that impact the characters and the plot."

That means research (see chapter 23 for more on research techniques). Beginning novelists tend to veer toward two extremes. One group does lots of great research, but includes all the research in their novels. "If the research doesn't fit the plot or character, don't include it," says Green. "If historical information is needed, put it at the beginning or end as an author's note. It's more rare to need to share before the story begins, but two authors who have done it well are Heather Day Gilbert in her Viking novel *Forest Child* and Kimberley Woodhouse in *The Mayflower Bride*."

The second trap is not doing enough research. Novelists may read a book or two or visit a couple of websites and call it good. "I don't even begin to write until I have read close to two dozen books related to my chosen slice of history," said Green. "I always find things in those books that directly impact the plot. And I always look for primary sources."

She has used diaries and memoirs to discover the price of groceries during the Civil War years, weather and climate, and food coming up in the garden. She's found lyrics from popular songs of the era. Green also discovered passenger lists from ships that carried young women from a prison in Paris to be wives for the French colonists in Louisiana.

If site visits aren't an option, Green knows who to call to ask questions that she couldn't get answered in her research. She has called a museum curator for help with specific details about a battle site; called an archivist at the Virginia Library to ask about where a house in a character's social class and background might be located on the James River. Green has also called a professor of environmental studies in New Orleans to understand what the geography of the area would have been like in 1721.

"It's a very slippery slope if we're all copying each other's novels. Historical novelists have a responsibility to make things as historically accurate as possible," said Green.

Some historical details to look for in your research: food/recipes, plays/operas, herbal remedies, mourning customs, transportation, local vegetation, games/entertainment, common illnesses, music, weather/climate, insects, and wildlife.

After reading endless historical fiction and researching and writing seven of them herself, Green has created a list of the best characteristics of an excellent historical novelist.

1. Loves learning. "If you don't love learning, you'll take shortcuts in research and present a book to readers without enough historical integrity," said Green.

2. Good storyteller. "I've read novels by people who have doctorates in the subject matter, but who were not great storytellers," she said.

3. Has a passion for the time period. "If you can't answer why your setting matters today, you're going to have a hard time being

motivated to finish the novel," said Green. "If you don't believe in the relevance that time period has to readers, why will anyone else?"

4. Curious. A curious writer does great research and digs deep for interesting and useful details.

5. Patient. A patient writer takes time to flesh out historical details and craft a great novel.

6. A detective. Search for clues to good research materials and sleuth out those little-known facts.

7. A detail person. "Details matter," said Green. "It all goes back to anchoring your reader in the story world. I'm thrilled when I hear readers say they were actually in the story, how they looked up and were surprised they were in their living room."

8. A journalistic background. This isn't mandatory, but a journalist learns quickly how to locate sources and background material, add interesting details, and tell the story.

Green also has good advice for beginning historical fiction writers. First, read good historical fiction and make notes about what makes one book good and another one not. Second, start with one excellent historical source book. Use its end notes to find other books, and so on. Third, make a site visit if possible. And finally, don't take shortcuts in your research.

"In *Widow of Gettysburg* I had a scene in which the protagonists heard cicadas. My editor wasn't sure cicadas could be heard at the time of day and year, so I called an entomologist to find out," said Green. "Yes, cicadas would have been heard then."

Despite all the research, occasionally things slip through. "When that happens, it keeps me humble," said Green.

••• Visit jocelyngreen.com •••

## Assignments

1. Think about the setting for your historical novel. Why does that setting matter to today's readers? What about that time period is important to readers now?

2. Where do you lean: too much research or not enough? Why or why not? What prevents you from deepening your novel with research?

3. List the characteristics of a good historical novelist that you feel you have. Which ones must you develop or expand on?

4. Create an itinerary for a site visit, including names of area museums, historical buildings, nearby archives and other places to see and

experience. If you know you can't go, begin searching for materials about the area available to purchase or borrow, including documentaries, brochures, maps, and books.

5.  How might your characters interact with the history going on during the time of your novel? Make a detailed chart of the events going on at that time, including how your character will react to those events. Examples: food shortages in WWII France; fashion trends in Regency England; prohibition in Chicago.

# Love Lines:
# The Heartbeat of Christian Romance

**26**

## GAIL GAYMER MARTIN

Gail Gaymer Martin is one of the matriarchs of the Christian romance genre. She is a founder of American Christian Fiction Writers and author of nearly 60 novels and novellas that all contain no small measure of love.

"Just as Jesus told stories that answered questions we have as humans, I write modern-day parables that answer questions readers have," said Martin, who lives in Arizona.

"A romance is the story of two people who fall in love, but they are flawed, damaged, and have problems that we all deal with as humans," she said. "Their flaws and issues keep them apart but eventually, through a willingness to look at their hearts and minds and deal with the issues, the romance happens."

Martin started writing Christian romances later in life, after teaching for nine years and working as a school counselor for 23 years. She began her new career writing church materials in 1994 while still working, moving quickly to magazine articles, devotionals, and poetry. By 1996 she was writing fiction full-time.

"I sent my first novel to Barbour; they loved my voice but couldn't use the story because I had an alcoholic husband in it. They asked if I had anything else," she said. "I rewrote my first novel, sent it in and got a contract in 11 days."

That first novel came out in 1998, a second in 1999. Her first contract with Love Inspired came in 1999, with the book out in 2000. She's been writing romance nonstop ever since. She's still writing for Love Inspired, for Winged Publication, Forget Me Not, and has had her work appear in anthologies published by Barbour.

The main ingredients to a good romance, said Martin, are the main characters.

"Make them as real as you can; look into their hearts and investigate what makes them real people," she said. "They are people who have been hurt, succeeded, and failed."

She encourages writers to create the characters' backstory, discovering what kind of family they were raised in, any financial dysfunction, illnesses, their faith stories. Perhaps the character is a Christian but deeply flawed, or is a Christian but walked away from faith, or knows about faith but hasn't taken it to heart.

"Create the backstory for yourself. Some of it may appear in the novel, but much won't," she said. "But what happened in the past certainly reflects on who we are today, and a character's backstory influences his or her feelings and actions."

The second key to a great romance is giving the characters options. "Give them two roads they can follow and have them choose," said Martin. "I'm surprised sometimes because characters pick a different option than I thought. A character will do something and I'll wonder why. Then I'll figure out why and the reason deepens my story."

A third key is establishing goals for the main characters. What does that character want? What does he or she need? Have a reason for the goal and the motivation. For example, say your main character wants a big promotion so he can earn more money to help his aging parents. But if he gets the promotion, his job will keep him away more often from his parents. Then he meets his parents' home health aide, who happens to own the business and who is mighty attractive. Her goal is to provide his parents with the best care possible, and that means having their son home more often. See? The goals clash, the romance blossoms, and somehow they choose the option that brings them together.

"Goals can change too," said Martin, "depending on how the romance works out."

Martin has a sound suggestion for Christian writers working on a romance novel. Instead of making everyone handsome or beautiful, try making them presentable but with positive attributes.

"Sometimes romance writers miss something with their characters: the attributes or characteristics that make them human," she said. "We need to be looking at our characters' heart and soul, not just their bodies. Make them more than just beautiful."

Martin has seen changes in the romance genre. There was a time when characters couldn't be divorced; now divorced main characters are allowed. Still, in Christian romance the discussion of body parts—breasts, thighs, sexual body parts—is taboo. There can be excitement and trembling bodies and throbbing hearts and even deepening kisses. But wait for the first kiss until roughly the middle of the book and forget the tongue.

Also, no swearing; no bedroom scenes; be careful with alcohol use; don't name a particular church denomination; no provocative clothing. And don't forget the happy ending.

"A Christian romance usually ends in marriage or a marriage proposal and acceptance," said Martin. "Romance has to have a happy ending, otherwise it wouldn't be romance. People read romance because they want a happy ending."

Martin's best advice is to write real. Christian fiction isn't a book filled with sitting in church, reading the Bible, singing hymns, and doing good deeds. Give your characters a Christian worldview, but have them live their lives like everyone else does.

"We have to make romances interesting and moving but without bedroom scenes, and that makes it harder to write," said Martin. "Christian romance needs lot of conflict, tension, and emotion."

••• Visit gailgaymermartin.com •••

## Assignments

1. Create the backstory for the main characters in your Christian romance. What was their childhood like? What tragedies did they have? What are they facing now?

2. What are your characters' goals? List three goals for each character and how those goals might bring your characters together or keep them apart.

3. Where do your characters stand regarding faith? Create a faith journey for each one, including where they have been, are now, and need to be.

4. Where have you crossed the line as far as physical contact between your characters? What must you change or improve?

5. Reread your novel, then figure out how to deepen the conflict, ratchet up the tension, and heighten the emotion.

# Writing for Children, Tweens, and Teens

# Children's Market:
# An Editor's Point of View

**27**

LINDA HOWARD

Linda Howard has spent years figuring out what parents are interested in, what children love, what book formats customers want, and what retailers want to sell in their stores.

The answers are pretty much the same: Don't give us the same old Bible stories in the same old ways. Give us new formats, new ways to tell the stories, something unique and different.

Howard is an associate publisher for Tyndale Kids, after rising through the ranks at the company where she's worked for about a decade. She and her team are working hard to provide consumers what they want.

"Tell us the great Bible stories, but tell them in a different way," she said. "In this age of digital everything, kids are entertained all the time. We're trying to find fun ways to tell the stories because there are other places kids can go to have fun. We're trying to keep up, just as every publisher is, because we're competing against things like interactive apps."

Howard said she turns down at least 95 percent of the projects she sees. "It's the part of my job I dislike the most; I feel responsible to be respectful and honest in the most positive way I can," she said. "I try to send some sort of critique to help these potential authors."

That 95-percent rejection rate reflects common mistakes potential authors make. She has several recommendations for those who dream of writing for children.

1. Have an agent. It's not that she doesn't accept books from authors without an agent; it's that an agent helps vet stories before sending and helps authors create the best book possible. She also

encourages writers to have a professional children's writer look over their work to spot potential problems.

2. Read your story aloud, especially if it's written in rhyme, before sending. "Your story may sound great in your head, but when you read aloud you'll find where it doesn't flow or doesn't work," said Howard.

3. Know how hard it is to write for children. "Some think that because a book is for kids that it's easy to write or that the kids won't care anyway," she said. "But kids are probably more discerning readers than adults."

4. Don't send illustrations. She cringes when she sees a project that is already designed for her. "A writer can get caught up in what they picture, but they're not design experts. I have a design department and an art director with 20 plus years of experience," she said. "We have a stable of quality illustrators who are professionals."

5. Research the company. Howard gets lots of projects that have no connection to what Tyndale publishes. "Take time to really look at where you're sending your project. Know where it fits," she said.

Howard and her team assess possible projects on three criteria. First is whether the project fits with Tyndale's overall mission and the specific mission of Tyndale Kids.

- Tyndale Mission Statement: Minister to the spiritual needs of people primarily through literature consistent with biblical principles.

- Tyndale Kids: Continuing Tyndale's rich heritage, we make God's Word more accessible to families by providing engaging, biblically based content for children and youth.

"Any project must go through those lenses. Does it meet our vision and mission?" she said.

Second, she looks at whether the author has a platform to help put their books out there. "We can do all the marketing in the world, but we've found, especially today, that authors sell books as much as marketing sells books," said Howard.

Third is whether the author is a good writer. "Will they engage the children and will they engage the parents? We're really looking for things that will reach the whole family," she said.

Howard offers good advice to writers:

- Visit stores (digital and brick-and-mortar) to see what's out there, what works, and what doesn't. You may find that your idea has been done 20 times already.

- Be creative in how you tell your story. Come at it from a different perspective.

Find a mentor who knows what he or she is doing. Be willing to pay for help.

Go to writers conferences. "Any education and continued learning about the craft is good," she said. "Don't ever think you've arrived; you can always learn something new."

Howard acquires book for all categories in the children's market, from board books to books for teens. But selling Young Adult (YA) books in the Christian market is "holy cow hard."

"Writing for the YA market is a subtle art," she said. "You've got to be so creative in how you bring your story to a publisher. You have to look at things in a fresh way, it's got to have a great Christian message without cramming it down your readers' throats."

She'd love to publish 5 to 8 books a year for tweens (ages 8–12) but hasn't found the right fit yet, and hasn't found much yet for the YA market.

"Our sales team says YA books have to be over-the-top good or don't do it," said Howard. "I'm not willing to abdicate this area yet because we have to bring things to that age group. We want to provide alternatives, to get good Christian teaching out there."

••• Visit tyndale.com/kids •••

## Children's Book Summit

A recent Children's Book Summit held in New York City was the venue for NPD BookScan's report on the growth of children's publishing in the religious market. BookScan was owned by Nielson, a well-known market research firm, before it was purchased by NPD Group. The Children's Book Summit is held annually and attended by religious and general market publishers.

The report revealed that children's book sales in the religion category jumped 22 percent from 2013 to 2016. That same report said that 11 of the top 20 best-selling 2015–16 religion titles were board books and six were Bible storybooks.

Consequently, some children's book publishers such as Harvest House, Tyndale Kids, and Westminster John Knox are expanding their children's lines. Others, such as Zondervan and B&H Kids, are even more strategic about their brands and publishing choices.

Byle, Ann. "Religion Publishers See Growth in Children's Books." May 10, 2017. *Publishers Weekly*. https://www.publishersweekly.com/pw/by-topic/industry-news/religion/article/73547-religion-publishers-see-growth-in-children-s-books.html

## Assignments

1. If your book is for children, read it aloud. Mark where it seems to stumble over word choice, rhythm, or concept. Now have someone else read it aloud and mark where he or she stumbles.

2. Assess and rewrite those stumbling points.

3. Research three publishing houses you think might fit your work. Look over mission statements, backlist, new titles, and new authors to see if you and your work match.

4. Visit a Christian or general market bookstore and spend time perusing the shelves and reading books in your genre. Make a list of popular topics, styles, and formats. Talk to a bookseller to learn what sells best and what kids like most (not always the same).

5. Research several writers conferences that may offer opportunities to meet mentors; also visit the websites of children's authors you admire. Who seems to be a good fit? How might you initiate contact with them?

# Making It Real:
# Writing for Tweens and Teens

28

NANCY RUE

Nancy Rue has been writing for tweens and teens for nearly 35 years. While technology and society has changed dramatically in those years, the core of her message hasn't.

"The things that tweens deal with now are the same core things they dealt with then," said Rue. "For girls, it's a sense of belonging—How do I fit in? For boys, it's How do I be a man, be strong, and make my mark? In the teen years, it's Who am I? Where am I going? What do I look like in others' eyes? Will I be okay?"

Rue has written 123 books, with all but 11 for tweens or teens. She began writing at age 30 after teaching high school English in her 20s. She's seen changes in education, with schools not as wonderful as they once were thanks to more violence, bullying, and pressure.

Older teens don't have as much hope now as they search for jobs that are hard to find, and realize that they can't expect the same level of success as their parents. And those parents are much more protective these days, so kids are less independent because parents fear for their safety.

Rue also says that kids' worlds tend to be dark, thanks in part to what society has allowed us to put on TV, in movies, and on the radio. They are much more privy to sexual issues and deep psychological issues. Not to mention that kids don't actually speak when they communicate—thanks to technology.

"One thing that has stayed constant is that I still love that 12 to 17 age group. I love the possibility, the potential," she said. "It's so much fun to watch them embrace truth and go forward. It's hard to watch them struggle, but I'm honored to be part of that struggle."

She also loves tweens, kids ages 8 to 12 who are dealing with harder stuff than ever before. There is flat-out intentional meanness and bullying, and her writing reflects that. She once wrote about friendship flubs and everyday issues but is now dealing with topics such as bullying and abuse.

"My approach has always been to make it real; it's about the big picture, the light and the dark together," said Rue. "I always try to weave Christian principles into my stories rather than paste them in. I want to be real and be authentic."

The Internet has been to her advantage. She started Tween You and Me (tweenyouandme.typepad.com) for tweens and In Real Life (tweenyouandme.typepad.com/in_real_life) for teen girls. "In creating these communities where it's safe to make comments, I'm finding out way more about their lives than if I had been meeting them in person," said Rue. "These kids are very transparent and brave, and I'm learning tons about what their lives are like."

There's more to writing for tweens and teens than deciding you want to. How hard can it be, you say? Wrong, says Rue.

"Are you hanging out with kids? When they cry, do you cry?" she asks. "You can't write down to kids. You have to get in there and get some of it on you."

Other questions for potential writers in this market: Do you love kids? Are you trying to straighten them out? Would you rather have lunch with them than adults? Do you enjoy being with them? Are you playing like a kid? Do you have an ear for how tweens and teens talk?

"One of the hardest things for writers is to get the dialogue right, but the narrative parts also have to sound like kids," said Rue. "A writer has to have a natural voice, and you can't teach voice. As soon as we start writing like writers, we lose the kids."

She has good advice for writers who are dedicated to writing for the teen or tween audience, gleaned from her years as a writer and her From Shadow to Shelf mentoring program (fromshadowtoshelf.com).

"First, try to focus on writing the book of your soul; focus on writing a book that is amazing," she said.

Second, once the book is written begin finding ways in which you are comfortable reaching out to your target audience through social media. And third, do whatever you must to not get discouraged.

"If that means finding a group of people who support you or a group of three or four girls who you read your story to, then do it. Do whatever you can to not be discouraged," said Rue. "Do everything you can to maintain a good attitude, and everything you can do to write the best book possible."

Her first mentoring client had met with a reputable Christian agent, who said she wasn't ready yet. That author began Nancy's mentoring program, fine-tuned her manuscript, won some awards with it, and got to know the right people in the publishing industry. The third book in her YA trilogy came out in 2016.

"It really can happen," said Rue. "Write about how things are, not how you think they should be. And find your voice. This is always essential, but especially so when writing for teens and tweens."

Rue is working on several projects these days, including the e-book *The Whole Christian Thing* and a book for parents called *Just Ignore It: Things We Should and Shouldn't Say to our Kids about Bullying*, which she'll do as an e-book and a series of podcasts. She is also developing a school program with author Tim Schumaker called "How to Be a Hero," which focuses on how to be a person who doesn't bully, isn't bullied, and doesn't stand by and let others bully.

"Writing for tweens and teens is about getting inside a character's skin," she said. "It's total immersion in kids' hearts, world, and heads. When you find that, it's a gift."

••• Visit nancyrue.com •••

## Assignments

1. Where and how are you spending time with teens or tweens? List places and ways you come in contact with them, either in person or via social media.

2. What is your goal for writing your teen/tween novel? Is it to fix kids or speak with them and into their lives? List your top reasons for writing for this market.

3. What are you doing to reach this market? Blogging? Interacting on social media such as Instagram or Snapchat? What are your numbers? Now decide where you can improve your social media reach.

4. List three or four adults and the same number of teens/tweens who you can ask to read your novel. Ask for specific suggestions, then apply their suggestions.

5. Describe your voice, especially as it reaches into this market. Ask others to describe your voice. Do the descriptions match? Why or why not?

# Writing for Children: Advice from the Expert on Rhythm, Rhyme, and Ideas

**29**

## CRYSTAL BOWMAN

Crystal Bowman has often heard how easy it must be to write a children's book. The books are short, fun, easy to read and have lots of pictures. How hard can it be, right? Wrong.

"In reality it's harder to write children's books because there are fewer words, vocabulary has to be at age-appropriate levels, and you have to express the ideas creatively and concretely," said Bowman.

Bowman has written board books, picture books, devotionals, I Can Read books, books of poems, song lyrics, and just about anything else children read. She's published with multiple publishers and some of her books have sold a million or more. Among her most recent books are *Our Daily Bread for Kids, Our Daily Bread for Preschoolers, Does God Take Naps?* and *Do Baby Bears Have Mommies?* all with her daughter Teri McKinley.

Bowman describes several general rules for writing for children.

"Any writer has to understand the cognitive levels of development in children," said Bowman, who has studied Piaget's developmental levels in depth. "Writers have to know the ages and stages a child goes through; they need to understand their physical, emotional, and intellectual development."

Knowing these developmental levels means avoiding rookie mistakes. One such mistake is including concepts like faith, but offering no explanation.

"You can't just say Abraham had faith," said Bowman. "Children don't understand what faith is so you have to offer concrete details, something like, 'Abraham had faith that God would lead him to a new home.'"

Another no-no is metaphor. "Kids are very literal," she said. "If you say, 'I had butterflies in my stomach,' meaning you were nervous, a child will think you actually have butterflies flying around your stomach."

Some of the biggest mistakes are using vocabulary that isn't age appropriate, using vague words, making the story too long, and making the voice too adult.

"People think they can just write a children's book and get it published," she said. "But for anything you do professionally, you have to have training. Why not in writing for children?"

## Rhythm and Rhyme

Rhythm and rhyme are the hardest to write. "You have to have a natural ability to write in rhythm and rhyme," she said. "You can improve your skills, however, so if you believe you have a natural talent, seek out an expert who can help you polish those skills."

Bowman—who often writes books in rhythm and rhyme—is the first to admit that she's still improving her craft. Over the last 20 years she's mentored writers, offered advice, taught at conferences, and read many, many manuscripts. There are a number of common errors when writers try rhythm and rhyme.

First is letting rhyme drive the writing. This makes for forced rhymes, awkward sentence structure and inconsistent rhythm. Rhythm is the cadence of the word or line, marked by the syllables of a word that each have a beat. Proper rhythm makes for a smooth, lyrical flow to the words, sentences, and stanzas.

She suggests using exact rhyme 99 percent of the time, and near rhymes rarely only if they fit the context.

Exact Rhymes: door/floor; try/fly; sad/glad; swing/sing; sneeze/please.

Near Rhymes: down/around; find/mine; friend/been; home/along; trash/grass.

Forced rhyme:
> "Samantha Sue,
> get up today!
> It's time for school,"
> my mother did say.

Natural rhyme:
> "Samantha Sue,
> get out of bed.
> It's time for school,"
> my mother said.

Awkward structure, improper grammar:
> To the park we all did go
> And oh, how we did love it so.

"Writers make a mistake when they throw grammar and sentence rules out the window. Learn the rules of writing in rhythm and rhyme, and stick with them. Keep the language natural; write how you talk," she said. "Poorly written rhythm and rhyme is the fastest way to the slush pile."

Many publishers, she said, say they don't accept books written in rhythm and rhyme. That doesn't mean they don't publish them; the publisher has a few people they trust for such books, and constantly go back to those authors who do rhythm and rhyme well.

"If rhythm and rhyme look easy, that's because it was done well," she said.

Bowman offers advice for writing for the very young. "Young children like rhythm, rhyme, and repetition. The book has to draw a child in, has to interact with that child," she said.

Picture books are about content, message, purpose and takeaway. "A book can be about entertainment, but it has to be more. There needs to be a plot, a beginning-middle-end, some conflict or tension," she said. The tension could be a lost teddy bear or fear of the dark or questions about animals.

"The ending of a picture book has to be a surprise, humorous, or at least satisfying," she said.

One mistake writers (and publishers) make in the Christian market is making promises from God they have no business making. Examples include saying that God will always keep a child safe, or that there will always be enough food, or that bad things will never happen. Writers can't know or assume such things, and therefore shouldn't write them.

"Writers have to know how a child thinks and the emotions that can get in their heads," said Bowman. "There is huge responsibility that comes with writing for children."

Bowman also said children's books must be multidimensional. First comes the story, but then comes layers such as exploring colors, shapes, counting, animals, or other things. Consider *The Very Hungry Caterpillar* by Eric Carle. There is the tale of the hungry caterpillar, but also counting, colors, fruits, the life cycle of a caterpillar, the interesting page sizes. *Goodnight Moon* by Margaret Wise Brown has its lovely rhythm, but children also discover the moon as it moves, the darkening room, and the mouse on each page.

Bowman offers advice to those who dream of writing children's books.

1. Study classic picture books to see how they work. Read *Goodnight Moon, Where the Wild Things Are, The Pokey Little Puppy, Blueberries for Sal, Make Way for Ducklings,* the works of Eric Carle, Shel Silverstein, and Dr. Seuss. "Study them, pore over them. Read each one until you can't learn anything else," she said.

2. Solicit or hire advice from an experienced, professional children's book writer or editor, and be prepared to pay for it. "Just because

friends and family think your book is good doesn't mean it is. Their opinions don't really matter because they aren't professional writers or editors," she said.

3.  If mentors, other writers, and editors say the same thing or offer the same advice about your work, *listen*. Change your work as necessary.

4.  Attend a writers conference where there will be professional children's book writers and editors. Take their workshops and learn from them.

Tap into resources for children's writers such as the Society for Children's Book Writers and Illustrators (scbwi.org), books including *Children's Writer's Word Book* by Alejandra Mogilner and blogs such as the Christian Children's Authors blog (christianchildrensauthors.com).

••• Visit crystalbowman.com •••

## Assignments

1.  Find Piaget's Stages of Cognitive Development and write a synopsis of each stage.

2.  Either buy or borrow a copy of *Children's Writer's Word Book* and compare the words you use in your book to what this resource recommends. Are you above age or below age level? Change words accordingly.

3.  Get copies of at least 10 classic children's books. Read each one five times and record what you notice about each one (e.g., word choice, multiple levels, artwork, story line, tension). How does your work compare?

4.  Read over your work and look for concepts (such as faith or liberty) that children won't understand. Look for metaphors and other references children won't understand. How can you change these?

5.  Compare your rhythm and rhyme to the criterion here, and/or to several of Bowman's books or other rhyming/rhythmic tales. What did you discover about your work? Should you be writing in rhythm and rhyme?

# Board Book Learning Curve: Little Books with Big Messages

## 30

GARY BOWER

Gary Bower has a built-in test audience for his board books and picture books. He has 12 children—seven are married—and 24 grandchildren.

"It's not hard to get into the mindset of my audience. I become a kid when I'm writing," said this prolific author who started his writing career with self-published books he and his wife, Jan, sold through craft and homeschool fairs.

He wrote and designed the books, which were illustrated by his wife. Bower has since moved into traditional publishing, with A Faith that God Built picture book series with Tyndale Kids and a board book series with WorthyKids/Ideals.

"I spend a lot of time talking to little kids," he said. "I like to get in kids' heads. I'll write a little ditty—something catchy and sing-song—and I never think it's childish. I think, *I like that!*"

He wrote many board books before ever publishing board books, filing the manuscripts away in hopes that they would eventually find life.

"You really have to craft a book. You have to make it sound natural and pleasant, to roll off the tongue," said Bower. "You have to work hard to make it sound like it didn't take a lot of work."

Board books are one of the fastest growing segments of the children's market for Christian publishers, according to NPD BookScan's report at a recent Children's Book Summit (https://www.publishersweekly.com/pw/by-topic/industry-news/religion/article/73547-religion-publishers-see-growth-in-children-s-books.html). Authors looking to write for children can find success with these little books that little hands can't tear up.

Bower suggests that the popularity of board books can be found in the price, which tends to be much lower than picture books, and in the length of a board book: they are quick reads that match the attention spans of children—and their parents.

"If you're writing a board book, keep it simple and basic. It has to be something children will like—faces, animals, colors—and the parents have to like it too. Add a little bit of humor that the kids won't get but the adults will," he said.

Board books have to taste good to the kids, according to Bower. Not tasty cardboard, but a feeling that the book is lively and enjoyable.

"Board books need to have a primary, clear purpose that's obvious," he said. "It can also work to add other, subtle things."

Think about *Goodnight Moon* by Margaret Wise Brown, which is available in board book form. Little Bunny is going to bed, but children can also find the mouse on each page, watch the colors darken and the moon move. Think also about a board book with counting as its primary purpose, but that adds colors and mama and baby animals. Or an ABC board book that uses a Bible story to illustrate the letters. There are several layers to each book, which makes it more endearing to children and adults.

Young children have a limited attention span, so excellent illustrations and well-written words are key to helping hold a child's attention. "The book should have a pleasing feel to it—a melody combined with colorful illustrations and cute facial expressions," said Bower.

Bower has good advice for those considering writing board books.

1. "Write what you enjoy," said Bower. But know that it won't always be easy. He struggles over words and phrases to make each one perfect. "Each word has to be strong on its own," he said.

2. Keep at it. "It takes hard work to make something simple be both endearing and high quality," Bower said. He writes and rewrites, sometimes putting a book away for a while to give himself a break before starting again.

3. Don't go for board books because you think it will be easy. "Fewer words don't make it easier; in some ways writing fewer words makes in harder," said Bower.

4. Read lots of board books, not to copy their styles but to learn from them. "Some board books are tremendous and don't do well; some do well for reasons I don't know; and some just do well. We can probably learn from all three," he said.

5. Hang out with kids. Bower's got a built-in crowd of youngsters, but other writers may have to search out children. "Find out what they love, find out what they ask for again and again and put that in a book," he said.

For Christian writers writing for the Christian market, creating a board book that reaches the soul of a child is a worthy goal.

"I'd rather sell 10,000 books that point a little one to Jesus than 1 million nonsense books," said Bower.

He also has advice for those considering self-publishing a picture book or board book.

"I believe in self-publishing—I've done it myself—but I strongly caution authors who want full color, library binding, full-page bleeds for their books. It's such a competitive market, and it's hard to get it printed and bound well for a reasonable price," said Bower. "There is so much labor involved and not a lot of money."

••• Visit bowerarts.com •••

## Reference Tools

Gary Bower uses these reference books as he writes for children:

- *Writing for Children and Teenagers*, by Lee Wyndam, revised by Arnold Madison.
- *Creating Characters Kids Will Love*, by Elaine Marie Alphin.
- *The Children's Writer's Reference*, by Berthe Amos and Eric Suben.
- *Children's Writer's Word Book*, by Alejandra Mogilner.

## Assignments

1. Gather about 20 board books and read each one. Look for patterns, similarities, topics, differences. Record your findings.

2. Gather board books with a Christian theme and study how each one addresses faith topics. Concrete terms? Abstract? Illustrations? Record your findings.

3. Ask yourself why you want to write board books. Make a list of five reasons why this genre appeals to you.

4. Read over your board book manuscript(s). Does it have one clear purpose/message? Does it flow nicely?

5. Check out from the library or purchase the reference books listed. Read through them to see how your book compares. Rewrite as needed.

# Drawing Attention:
# The Importance of Good Illustrations

31

KENNETH KRAEGEL

Amateur musician. Theology student. Refugee resettlement worker. Developmental disabilities worker. Organic vegetable farmer. And finally, children's book writer and illustrator.

Kenneth Kraegel has had a rich and varied journey to his destination as a multi-published, much-lauded children's book writer and illustrator. His first picture book, *King Arthur's Very Great Grandson*, came out in 2012, followed by *The Song of Delphine* and *Green Pants*. He always has new books in the works.

While he hasn't had a formal art-school education, Kraegel has a lifetime of learning and experience. He knows what works for him, what his publisher likes, what children love, and how to blend all that into a picture book that delights readers of all ages.

"With each book I have to shed off another layer of arrogance and build up another layer of trust in the people I work with," said Kraegel. "Editors and art directors do this all day and they really do know what they're talking about."

Once he has a story in mind, Kraegel creates preliminary sketches for each page, eventually making a dummy book with story and sample illustrations. He creates the first sketches for the book, then puts them on a light box and fleshes them out with watercolors. At this stage, he adds or subtracts from the drawing. He likes to do all this work before sitting down to create the final watercolor illustration.

"I've learned to simplify my illustrations," said Kraegel. "I like to add a lot of detail, but I've learned to allow more open space in my books. I hint at details rather than drawing them out. The details need to be in the reader's mind, not crowding an illustration."

139

Kraegel says that good illustrations in a children's book always add to the story.

"Illustrations should *enhance the story*, not just create a picture of what the words say. An illustration is adding details to the setting or the characters," he said.

Also, particularly in books for prereaders, pictures must be fun to look at—fun enough to draw them back again and again.

"Illustrations need to be readable, with *emotions and actions conveyed directly* enough for kids to know what's happening and what characters are feeling," said Kraegel.

He also points to the composition of the page.

"Illustrations must sit well with the text; there should be a flow and a *feeling of naturalness* to where everything is placed on the page," Kraegel said. "You can arrange a tree and a dog and a basketball hoop on a page in so many different ways. I spend a lot of time playing around with the basic shapes in an illustration."

If he wants to convey tense feelings, he crowds things together. He spreads the elements apart for a more serene feeling.

Also key to a good illustration is how the action is represented. Action should move from left to right, which is how we read and turn pages; and they should also occur away from the gutter and page edges. "The trick with picture books is you always have the gutter where pages meet. Don't put anything important within a half inch on either side of the gutter, or within a half inch of the edges of the page," he said. It's like a puzzle, he added, figuring out how to place everything on a page so it doesn't feel crowded or lose important elements near the gutter, edges or even the text.

Each illustration should have a fullness, a *sense of completeness*, according to Kraegel, whether a two-page spread or a spot illustration. "Every illustration should have a sense of coherence. Each one needs to be solid and needs to look like it is a legitimate part of the book," he said. "And those small illustrations take just as much work as a bigger one."

Want to create bad illustrations? Create inconsistent characters and draw a picture of exactly what the words are saying. "It takes a certain level of ability to draw characters as exactly the same person doing bunches of different things," he said. "Too much variation in characters isn't good; looking at whether you can draw *consistent characters* is one way to know if your illustrations are good enough to be published."

## Advice for artists

Kraegel offers advice for artists who want get into illustrating children's books:

"For those starting out, find people you trust to share your work with. Find people who can show you where your strengths are, who can show you where you might need work," he said.

Conferences are great places to get straight feedback from editors, as well as meet people you might form a relationship with to critique work. Again, find people you trust to offer honest feedback.

Another way to see how your work measures up is to compare it to published books by a variety of illustrators. Do you have the same quality and depth as these published authors? Compare your work to both old classics and new books, searching out Caldecott Medal winners and honorable mentions, as well as those that the children in your life return to again and again.

His favorites are books by Maurice Sendak, Dr. Seuss, Robert McCloskey, Chris Van Allsburg, and the Frog and Toad books by Arnold Lobel.

Second, develop a solid portfolio of illustrations that demonstrate your ability. He suggests creating a dozen illustrations of the same character in different settings doing different things. "Publishers need to know you can reliably create good pictures," Kraegel said.

He asks himself with each project how the book might be received. Is there something in the book that people won't understand or that won't appeal to them? He asks himself how people outside his circle will see the illustrations. Will they see their own ethnicities, see people with disabilities represented well, get the jokes?

"Good illustrations will *create a world*," said Kraegel. "With picture books you have the potential to create an engaging and interesting world that draws readers in and keeps them all—young and old—coming back."

••• Visit kennethkraegel.com •••

## Elements of Good Illustrations

1. Always enhance the story
2. Convey actions and emotions clearly
3. Flow with natural placement on the page
4. Keep action elements away from the edges, gutter and text
5. Present a sense of completeness in big and small art
6. Offer consistent characters throughout
7. Create a world

## Assignments

1. Gather picture books by Maurice Sendak, Dr. Seuss, Robert McCloskey, Chris Van Allsburg, and Arnold Lobel. Read through each book and see how it measures up to the Elements of Good Illustrations listed in the sidebar. Create a graph or list of how each book measures up (or doesn't); be specific.

2. Look at your most recent illustrations. How do they compare to the list in the sidebar?

3. Practice drawing the same character doing a variety of things such as playing in a tree house, jousting, swimming, sitting at a desk in school, or playing soccer. Is the character consistent in each drawing? Why or why not?

4. Research the Caldecott Medal, then find a dozen or so of the winners or honor books and study them. What draws you to them? How do your illustrations compare?

5. Begin creating a portfolio of your best work. Purchase a holder for physical illustrations and/or create a web page to display digital copies.

# Engaging with Kids: Turning Your Children's Book into Programs

**32**

KEVIN KAMMERAAD

Children's book authors have an open door to meeting their readers right where they are: sitting on the floor or at their desks listening to the author read from or talk about their books. Feedback is immediate and usually pointedly honest. Children's authors can tap into this ready critique service, occasionally make a little money, and meet the adults who are eager to purchase books that children love.

Kevin Kammeraad has created a steady, diversified income thanks to his programs that point audiences back to his books.

Kammeraad was attending Grand Valley State University in West Michigan, working toward a degree in film and video. He started writing funny poems and illustrating them, then putting them to music thanks to his connections with local musicians for whom he made promo videos.

The process of making his first book, *The Tomato Collection*, was more of a "huh, look what's coming together" than a sit-down-and-write-a-book affair. He had those funny poems he'd done, but not much else.

Then came the puppet. He hired a puppet maker to create one of the characters, Jacob, from *The Tomato Collection*.

"I still didn't know what I'd do with all of this, but I was required for a college class to read in three classrooms. Instead of reading typical children's lit, I read my own work," said Kammeraad. "I thought why not use the poems I'm working on?"

He specifically remembers getting a phone call from a different elementary school in the district asking him to visit and read his poems, and how much did he charge.

"I thought, *Woo hoo!* I was excited and thrilled that they asked. From there I started asking around about how this works. Could authors go to schools and do programs?" he said.

All this happened in the late 1990s, with Kammeraad quitting his job in January 1999, getting copies of *The Tomato Collection* in March 1999, and by fall 1999 overwhelmed with the number of school visits he had scheduled during the 1999–2000 school year.

He published more books, released music albums, made more puppets, and stayed mighty busy. He figures he's visited at least 1,000 elementary schools in the nearly 20 years since he started.

Kammeraad added family and Christmas programs at libraries, festivals, special events and churches. In 2011 he began participating in Art-Prize, the independent, international art competition that takes place in Grand Rapids, Michigan. His latest books are *Spinach Dip Pancakes* and *Wimee's Words: Vehicles and Colors*, for which he collaborated with his wife.

Writers of children's books have a wide open door to add performances to their writing repertoire. This successful performer has good advice for authors eager to find new ways to reach their young readers and the adults in their lives.

1. Make your program captivating. Connect to kids in a way that makes them want to be there and act upon what you're saying. For authors, you want to get kids excited about reading and writing.

"Just standing up there talking makes the kids bored, and they'll think writing is boring," said Kammeraad.

Kammeraad engages children with personal stories, music, singing, puppets, and a fair amount of zany fun. It works for him, but it may not work for every children's author.

"An author should ask him or herself if programs are right for you," he said. "If you think it could work, know that it takes time to develop programs. What I do now is very different from when I started. As you do more programs, you'll become more confident."

2. Watch other authors in action. See what they do and gain inspiration. Don't copy another's work, but use it to inspire your own.

3. Be flexible. "When the script isn't working and you don't know what to do, adapt," said Kammeraad. "Sometimes kids don't make a peep, other times it's chaos. Having multiple options that allow you to adapt comes with experience."

4. Don't charge when you start out. "Not charging removes the pressure for you to produce," said Kammeraad. "Gain experience before you begin charging, then ask around about going rates."

5. Ask for feedback. Ask teachers and adults in the classroom whether your program worked. Kammeraad decided several years ago to forego using PowerPoint, but made sure to ask teachers whether the program was still educational enough. They said it was. Conversations or comment sheets are good ways to get feedback.

6. Find out if props work for you and if so, which ones. "People bring me in as an author, which is the focus, but using music and puppets brings the program to life and makes it sustainable," said Kammeraad. "The kids will see through something you're uncomfortable with, so find your niche and exploit that to deepen your program."

7. Consider bringing in a partner. Know someone who plays guitar, does magic tricks, or makes puppets? Could they be part of your program? "What I do is much more effective when I work with people who can collaborate," he said.

8. Learn themes at schools and other venues and work to the themes, such as your state's history, holidays, values such as charity and respect, or seasons. Match your books to these themes if you can.

9. Interact with the audience. Ask questions, invite them to participate, or toss a ball back and forth.

10. Build your marketing skills. "My website, social media, and word of mouth has been the backbone for me," Kammeraad said. He suggests speaking at conferences, an email newsletter, physical mailing list, calls, letters of recommendations, endorsements, and lots of networking.

Kammeraad never said adding programs to your writing job would be easy. He's made mistakes along the way and has learned some lessons the hard way. Here are three mistakes to avoid as you consider this new level of engagement.

1. Making the program all about you instead of the kids. "The point isn't about you, but about motivating kids to be excited about writing. Support what teachers are doing in the classroom," he said.

2. Not seeing yourself as a role model. "Be aware that kids may see you outside of school, so live with them in mind. Wear your bike helmet or walk with a flashlight. Understand and appreciate the weight of that," he said.

3. Giving up too soon. "It'll be hard when you first start, especially if you haven't been speaking or performing. Don't be discouraged," he said.

••• Visit kevinkammeraad.com •••

## Assignments

1. How might you get involved with children's performances/programs based on your books or your love of writing? Does this excite you? Scare you? List the pros and cons of taking this additional step.

2. Create a list of themes based on your books on which you could base programs.

3. Consider what props you might include. Puppets? Music? Magic? Singing? Could someone help you?

4. Do you intend to reach into the public school market? Christian school market? How can you tailor your programs to reach both?

5. Make a list of performers and programs you can observe to get a feel for what they're doing and what kids like. Can you schedule a meeting to pick their brains? Tap into libraries, schools, and even YouTube to watch performances.

# Reaching Your Readers

# Building a Platform: Five Ways to Reach Your Readers

**33**

KATHI LIPP

"Platform" can seem like a dirty word for authors eager to get a book contract. Traditional publishers seem to want authors who reach tens of thousands via speaking, blogging, and social media. Even small houses look for authors with some sort of platform.

Authors may find help by thinking about platform another, more productive, way: reaching your readers and potential readers by offering them something they want and need. What can you give them that no one else can? How can you enhance their lives in some way?

Kathi Lipp has been helping authors think through their platforms and brands for years, teaching them via her own successes and failures. She offers these five ways for beginning writers to develop their platforms—and begin reaching their readers.

"You don't have to do all of these things, but you should do most of them after figuring out what works best," she said. "Figure out what you can be consistent with. If you can't learn to fall in love with platform, you're not going to do it."

**Speak.** Lipp suggests developing a speaking platform based on the topic of your nonfiction book or themes in your novel. Venues include MOPS groups, Kiwanis, Rotary, church groups, homeschool groups, Bible studies, and conferences. Topics vary based on book content and venue.

"Building a speaking platform is attractive to publishers who see you selling books at the back of the room," she said. "It shows a level of professionalism."

Learn more about speaking at organizations such as Toastmasters and at conferences such as Speak Up (speakupconference.com) and Leverage: The Speaker Conference (communicatoracademy.com/leverage/).

**Blog.** Lipp urges writers to blog with a purpose, offering readers great content in exchange for their attention and/or something of value when they sign up to receive your blog or email newsletter.

"Blogging is not just putting thoughts up there; it's getting people to choose to follow you," said Lipp. "The most basic way of doing that is to offer them something of value. For me it was a cookbook aimed at cooking for your husband." Lipp suggests putting a tool at the bottom of your blog to allow readers to opt in to what you offer.

Key, she said, is knowing who the audience is for your blog. Is it writers? Moms of special needs children? Lapsed Baptists? People with financial questions? Whoever it is, focus content specifically on that group.

Also consider periodically offering a gift on your blog via a contest or in exchange for signing up to receive email notifications or newsletters. The gift could be a free download of additional content, a free book, or a gift card.

But no constant selling! Readers get tired of constant shilling on your part. Offer content that serves your readers, with an occasional promotion when it ties organically to your content.

**Create community.** "Give people a place to meet and talk about your book," said Lipp. "Create a Bible study around your book; do a book club; create products that draw community." Lipp suggests gathering people on Facebook, your website, your blog, and even in person if you can. Have space for comments, then respond to those comments so readers know you're interested and engaged. And listen to your readers.

"Hear what your readers are asking for," said Lipp, "then give them what they want." The key is creating a place readers and fans can come to connect with people of like mind and interests. Those are the people who will read your blog and one day buy your book.

**Create a leader's guide.** Before her first book came out, Lipp was asked to speak at a MOPS convention about the book, titled *The Husband Project: 21 Days of Loving Your Man—on Purpose and with a Plan.* She didn't have books yet, so she created a leader's guide with discussion questions and other information and put it on a CD. She brought 200 to the conference, but ended up giving away 800 copies total. It's now a download on her website.

"It's leveraging content to increase awareness and sales," said Lipp.

Think about how you can take content you already have and add value to your readers through deepening that content. How might a book club, Bible study group, writers group, or group of friends use that additional content? Make it available on your website/blog and offer discounts for buying more than three copies.

**Use social media.** Lipp suggests picking two forms of social media and posting consistently, and have those posts point to your blog that has your offer. Facebook, Twitter, Instagram, Pinterest, Snapchat, and any number of others (staying away from the questionable ones) can draw readers to your valuable content.

Lipp offers suggestions about what to post: lists, fun jokes and stories, repost blog posts from others, graphics, share old blog posts. You can share funny things about your family that show your personality, but she warns against too much detail that might embarrass your family (or readers) or reveal private information.

It's all about consistency—with your social media posts and with your blog.

"Platform" isn't a dirty word for writers. Platform is a way to reach your readers with good content they can use. Some say it feels like self-promotion and whisper Proverbs 16:18: "Pride goes before destruction, a haughty spirit before a fall" (NIV).

"If you approach *platform* by asking how you can serve your readers, it takes the smarmy out," said Lipp. "Platform is the act of falling in love with your readers, and giving them the opportunity to fall in love with you."

••• Visit kathilipp.com •••

## Assignments

1. What are your feelings about the word "platform?" Positive or negative? Create a mission statement about your goals and methods for reaching readers.

2. Which of the five suggestions hits your sweet spot? Why or why not? Begin making a plan to start or restart these platform builders. Make a list of the resources you already have in place, skills you'll need to learn, and experts you'll need to talk to.

3. Who is your audience for your blog? Be specific; list the characteristics of this audience.

4. Make a list of specific content you can offer based on your book and your audience. How does this content benefit your readers? Be specific.

5. What social media platforms are you familiar with and do you use? How can you use them better and what more can you learn about each one?

# Post, Tweet, Blog:
# Using Social Media to Best Advantage

**34**

SUSIE FINKBEINER

Susie Finkbeiner started getting serious about social media at the same time she got serious about writing as a career. She knew that reaching her future readers was mandatory, so she began watching authors who were doing it well.

One of her models was Jason Boyett, author of *Oh Me of Little Faith: True Confessions of a Spiritual Weakling*. All his social media—then he was on Twitter, Facebook, and LinkedIn—pointed back to his website/blog, like spokes of a wheel attached to the hub. She also noticed that he was good at working with other nonfiction authors to promote each others' work.

That model became her game plan for both her personal social media and for Breathe Christian Writers Conference, for which she handles social media.

She blogs on her WordPress site two or three times a week, and mentions it on Facebook and Twitter. "I write a short blurb/teaser and include a link to the blog post; the teaser includes whatever art I include on the blog," she said.

She measures a 75-percent click-through from Facebook/Twitter to her blog when she includes a unique photo or design element. "My posts are more successful because the picture catches peoples' eyes," she said. "Using just my picture isn't anything different and it isn't bad, but art is unique."

Finkbeiner thinks a lot about what her content should look like. Is she offering content that her readers can use? Is her content new and fresh?

"I ask myself if my readers will be encouraged, will they laugh, will it be useful. For me as a fiction writer, my readers want to know who I am as a person and what motivates me," she said.

For example, she signed the contract for her novel *A Cup of Dust* at the Breathe Christian Writers Conference in October 2014. She posted pictures of her and Kregel editor Dawn Anderson on her website and social media; it was also seen on Breathe and Kregel social media, and social media for her literary agency Credo Communications. Reposts helped spread the word even more.

"The pictures captured that event for my loyal readership, and readers are always willing to root for their author," said Finkbeiner. "Sharing a picture of a landmark moment makes someone who may be 500 miles away feel like they are part of something. Ultimately, if they are going to hold that book in their hands, it's a process they got to be involved in."

She has a mission statement for her social media: "Building relationships with readers, connecting with them, and making them feel welcome in my world." But Finkbeiner doesn't share everything; in fact, she holds back quite a lot. She doesn't post pictures of her kids; doesn't talk about her marriage; keeps private stuff private.

"While you want to have the appearance of transparency, you don't give everything away. You have to have a personal life," she said. "We live in a time of over sharing, and that's not healthy."

Intentionality is key. "You can speak your mind, but you have to be careful. You don't want people to have negative feelings when they come to your page," said Finkbeiner. "You want them to leave your page feeling uplifted or encouraged or laughing or with good information. I don't want my social media readers to be irritated, offended, or feel like I think they are stupid."

She's seen people use their life experiences as a means to get attention, to get more retweets and blog hits. "It's tempting to exploit your life to get that extra click, but it's not worth it," she said. "You don't want to elicit pity from your readership because it's only so long before people get annoyed."

But you can use your life circumstances to talk about what you've learned or how you grew. "People want to see someone who is not living as a victim," said Finkbeiner. "Readers want to see people overcome, but nobody likes it when it's all about you."

Good social media is a careful blend of an author's personal and writing life. Finkbeiner offers suggestions for the types of things to post:

1.  Tell about what inspired you to write the book.

2.  Share information related to the topic of your book. Historical fiction novelist Jocelyn Green (see chapter 25) posts information about significant dates in the Civil War or figures on whom she based her characters.

3.  Offer giveaways, including copies of your book or friends' books. This is a good opportunity to cross promote.

4.  Give away an art piece related to your book. Finkbeiner commissioned an artist friend to do a painting associated with her novel *A Cup of Dust*.

5.  Offer recipes related to your book.

The most important thing, according to Finkbeiner, is to avoid "selling" your book in every post. "There is a fine line between exploiting social media to sell books and tasteful posts," said Finkbeiner. "When I feel like an author is trying to sell me something, I don't follow them anymore because it's annoying. But share with me new information or something you've learned and I'll follow you forever."

She has advice for authors just getting started.

- Don't be afraid to ask your friends to tell their friends about you. "Friends are eager to be loudspeakers, but they need to know you want them to," said Finkbeiner.

- Thank people when they repost or do something nice for you.

- Don't use someone else's platform unless they offer it to you.

- No coattailing! This is the ugly habit of posting on others' social media about your own book and linking to it. Ick.

"Social media etiquette says to not do online what you wouldn't do in real life," said Finkbeiner. "Don't insult people, start a fight, interrupt, call people names, don't show off about yourself. Basically, don't be a jerk."

If you want to make connections, she said, act like a decent human being and remember that social media "is a tool; it's not life."

••• Visit susiefinkbeiner.com and breatheconference.com •••

---

### Tips for Using Social Media

1. Know that the social media landscape has changed in that fewer people are commenting. They are reading, just not commenting all the time.

2. It's better to have a smaller group of loyal fans that follow you forever than a big bunch of flash-in-the-pan hits that never think about you again.

3. Social media is constantly changing, so you have adapt as well; don't get stale.

4. Each year look at your numbers and see what worked and what didn't, then try to reproduce what did work in a new way.

5. Know that social media numbers go down in the summer and around the holidays.

6. Think about the end game, not just today's numbers. Ask how what you're doing now is building relationships and name recognition for the future.

## From Blog to Book – Jami Amerine

Jami Amerine started her career by writing a nonfiction book, then started a blog that maybe 60 people read and got her in trouble because she wrote funny stuff about her foster children. She got so mad she wrote a novel, then attended the American Christian Fiction Writers conference where literary agent Jessica Kirkland suggested she write a blog. Amerine was back to square one.

Then she put up a post titled "An Open Letter to My Children: You're Not that Great." Her phone kept pinging the next day, which happened to be her birthday, as people read the blog post. She had a thousand views; within an hour she had 10,000; the next hour she had 15,000. By the end of that month, she had 600,000 views for that post and soon signed with Kirkland.

She received a two-book contract with Harvest House, with *Stolen Jesus: An Unconventional Search for the Real Savior* the first book to release. She got rave reviews, including a glowing Tweet from Kathie Lee Gifford.

Amerine has these suggestions for bloggers hoping to touch the hearts of readers:

1. Have a great title. "Titles are my superpower," she said. Hers are often countercultural, but they draw readers in.

2. Tell it like it is. "When I'm at my worst and have been honest about that, God reveals something. People want that camaraderie," she said. "When I reveal that I got into foster care so God wouldn't be mean to us instead of me being preachy and teachy, people want that."

"That first blog post [that went viral] isn't my best writing, but if I'd written it any other way it wouldn't have resonated," she said.

••• Visit sacredgroundstickyfloors.com •••

## Assignments

1. Study four authors whose social media—blog, website, Facebook, Twitter, Pinterest—you admire. What do you like about each one? Consider tone, content, layout, frequency.

2. Create a mission statement for your social media.

3. Based on your mission statement, list the content you could provide based on your book, expertise, life experiences, hobbies, and research.

4. Teach yourself how to measure the hits, likes, retweets, and reposts. Begin tracking which of your posts are most successful and which aren't. What do you think makes one successful and another not?

5. Set three goals regarding your social media to reflect where you'd like to be a year from now.

# Online Audit:
# Tracking your Digital Footprint

## 35

LINDSAY AND SCOTT GUSTAFSON
AND ALEXIS DE WEESE

Scott and Lindsay Gustafson spend their days tracking what their clients—often authors and publishers—are doing online, what that action says about the client, and who that client is reaching. They call it a digital audit.

"We do an assessment of all the places the author has a digital voice, and the narrative that voice is leaving in the digital realm," said the Gustafsons, who own Apricot Services in Grand Rapids, Michigan. "Authors and publishers may think they are telling one story, but they may be telling readers something completely different. We discover what they are really communicating."

This is no guessing game. Assessment tools, metrics, and a host of measuring devices can track who is reading what websites, who is following what blogs, and who is commenting on what postings. Tracking is done via Google analytics, kind of comments, number of shares and retweets, social media insights, sales numbers, number of followers, and market research.

"The measuring is very scientific, not just a guess," they said. "A publisher might think it is reaching women ages 25–45, but the stats reveal something totally different. Knowing these things helps authors and publishers open their eyes to changing their marketing tactics, voice, and digital reach."

Once the Gustafsons measure who an author is reaching and his or her digital footprint, they can help the author narrow digital focus and build the online persona that fits her best. They ask questions about why the author wrote his or her book, the voice she wants to project, and what is driving both the author and the digital audience.

"It's about finding the tribe that your message connects with," they said. "That's the passion we want to link to and that's where things happen in digital spaces."

The focus, they said, is the tribe and not the author. It's an incarnational model: "Instead of broadcasting your own content, try to find out how your audience hears that content and responds," they said. "Developing a relationship with your tribe leaves room for your personality to come out."

Personality leads to voice, and voice leads to deeper connection with your audience.

Finding your voice or "brand" online can help you connect with your audience and still be true to yourself. Alexis De Weese, project manager at Apricot, adds, "Brand is a promise to your audience—it is a way to tell them who you are, what you represent, and how you will interact with them." She also points out that "brands begin to take on the characteristics of people and the beauty of having a brand as an author is that a decent part of the brand—and your work—is you!"

De Weese recommends thinking through the demographics of your readers: age, gender, interests. How do they spend their time? How do they find their reading material? What digital channels do they pay attention to? Discover this information three ways:

1. Observation—Interview people who match your ideal follower, asking them questions about how they purchase, what they read, who they follow online.

2. Online research—Who else are your ideal readers following? What else is popular with this audience? What's trending in genres/companies related to yours? What content of yours has received unusually high response?

3. Peer research—Look at other authors or businesses and see how they are using their platforms to reach audiences. Is it effective? What can you learn?

"Authors and publishers think of social media as a tool to connect with an audience, but because they think of it as a tool they don't often give it enough attention," said the Gustafsons. "Social media is the most real connection you'll have with 95 percent of your audience. If an author takes time each day to post content, and when that content gets a response takes time to respond back, that is real connecting."

Connection is the key. "Social media is a good way to sift out those who just want to sell from those who see it as a privilege to deliver their content to their audience daily via social media," they said. "It isn't about just adding noise to the social media realm; it's about contributing to and encouraging lives."

The Gustafsons have identified three kinds of authors in the social media realm.

1. Silent authors who don't want to say anything for fear of offending or being perceived as a narcissist. Many Christian authors fall into this category, they say.

2. All-about-themselves folks who constantly push themselves onto their audiences instead of pulling those audiences to them. Think celebrities and many secular authors.

3. Engaged authors who want to serve their audiences.

It's not hard to figure out who is who, they said. The challenge for Christian authors is to move from the silent type to finding true connection in digital spaces.

Christian fiction authors can offer content related to their novels, but can also offer passion for their books. Think of it as bonus content on a DVD: behind-the-scenes looks at places or time periods connected with the book, why an author writes, how he writes, discussions on the art of fiction.

Nonfiction authors can offer their tribe additional content beyond the book, an article on a related topic, and their passion for writing the book.

While publishers are all about an author's platform, it's important for an author to see that building a platform is secondary to having content, knowledge, and passion.

"When it comes down to it, it's all about content marketing," said the Gustafsons, who encourage authors to continue to develop as a person and writer and to dig deep into topics they are passionate about. "If your digital platform is driven by the desire to get published (or stay published) instead of real desire to connect with your tribe and deliver content, it can appear fake and people can begin to tell."

They offer several pieces of advice for authors looking to discover what their digital footprint is.

1. Engage in social listening. "Use your digital ears to learn what people in the digital spaces are saying about you or your topic. Also, begin to comment on those who write about your topic," said the Gustafsons.

2. Write and share a wide variety of content, and don't forget the call to action (the call for reader to act in some way, such as donate, purchase, or make a life change). "Be a little more brave about a call to action on social media. If you put a 'sell' post out there about your book, make sure you offer your tribe a way to buy your book," they said.

3. Integrate your social media and website well with a branded voice.

4. Build your brand and reader personas. "Ask yourself if your brand and average reader were characters, who would they be and how

would they communicate," said De Weese. "The answer can inform a lot in a digital space."

5. Watch your competition. "Observe others writing in your genre or market space," she said. "What do you admire about their content? What don't you prefer? How might you apply this knowledge to your platform?"

••• Visit apricotservices.com •••

## Assignments

1. Do your own digital audit, or hire someone to do it for you. Who is visiting your site, following your blog, retweeting your posts, 'liking' you on Facebook? What does your digital presence really saying about you, and who are you really reaching?

2. How does your actual digital voice differ from what you thought it was? Who are you actually reaching compared to who you thought you were? Describe what you thought your voice was and what it really is; do the same with your audience.

3. Which kind of author do you think you are: silent, all-about-yourself, or truly engaging with your tribe? How can you change to become an author who truly engages with her audience? What will you do?

4. Create a list of topics—be specific—that you can write about to deepen the content on your social media platform.

5. Do a digital audit on an author whose social media you admire. What is he or she doing right? Track the posts you like and record why. Also do a digital audit on someone whose social media bugs you. Record what annoys you. What will you do differently on your own social media?

# Open Doors:
# Partnering with Christian Retailers

**36**

SUE SMITH

Much has been made about the demise of Christian retail stores. There is the astronomical growth of online shopping, the closing of several hundred Christian chain stores plus smaller independent stores, and a shrinking number of general market bookstores. But is it the end?

Sue Smith, manager of Baker Book House, an independent Christian retail store in Grand Rapids, Michigan, says no. Tapping into the power of an author's reach and the energy of Christian retail can yield big results for both.

"The best thing Christian retail can do is introduce the author and his or her writing to the community," said Smith, who is also on the board of CBA, The Association for Christian Retail.

Smith cites a number of benefits Christian retail stores can offer authors: hand selling books to customers; placement on shelves/end caps/display tables; blogging about the book/author on store social media; in-store events; Skype events.

"Hand selling is probably the biggest thing we can do, but partnering with an author on our social media is great too," said Smith. "When we're blogging about a book and that blog is connected to the author's social media, the community around the author expands."

All this isn't limited to authors who have a local Christian bookstore they can connect with. Baker Book House has held Skype interviews with novelists Wanda Brunstetter, Charles Martin, and others, inviting readers to come to the store to "meet" the author on screen. The store also holds in-store events for authors willing to travel (bookstores don't pay authors to come).

She urges authors to contact stores directly via phone or email, connecting at least two months prior to the hoped-for event with the person who coordinates events. Research stores first, learning as much as possible about the events they do, how often, the store's online presence, and staff. Most Christian stores work with minimal staff, so authors must do the legwork themselves.

Note: Authors published by traditional publishing houses will usually have a publicist who can make initial contact with stores. Encourage your publicist to do this, but follow up with the store yourself.

"Authors need bring not only their books, but their whole social media platform to the store," said Smith. "Come with your own marketing ideas. Tell them 'These are the people I can connect to your store.'"

There are a number of ways to connect readers to a specific Christian retail store, but also to Christian retail at large. First, shop Christian retail yourself either in person or online via a store's website. With so many stores closing, a Christian bookstore in your area isn't a given. Find the nearest one and order via its website if possible.

Also direct your readers to Christian retail. Instead of always listing Amazon as the first way to buy your book, encourage readers to buy or order via a Christian retailer and list the store's website.

Come up with your own unique events ideas. Sharon Brown, author of the Sensible Shoes series and a Grand Rapids-area resident, opened the first box of one of her books at the store. She and her fans saw it first at Baker Book House, and it was all over the store's and Brown's social media.

Smith has also pushed publishers to provide the store with early inventory of long-awaited books. She can then advertise that Baker Book House has the first and earliest copies of popular books—another way to draw customers to its physical and online store.

Smith presses the importance of bringing your own fans to events scheduled at a store. Baker Book House, for instance, can only do so much to promote your event (in-store posters and other signage, posting on its social media, occasional pre-event media coverage). You need to promote the event in your circles—your social media, church, friends, coworkers—to get as many people as possible in the doors.

"Think about what you can bring to the table, what you can bring to the store," she said. "Come with an attitude of humbleness and know something about the store."

First-time authors, especially those with custom- or self-published books, shouldn't expect the same level of event as well-known authors with big sales and fan bases. Christian retail is, after all, a business. Stores will break even at about two dozen book sales after accounting for money, time, and energy needed to promote and host an event which typically includes the author speaking and signing books in the store's event space.

Baker Book House offers, for $25, a chair and table by the front door for authors who would like to sell/sign books. For $50, an author gets posters and signage throughout the store; for $75, all of the above plus mention on the store's Facebook page. Books are vetted before a decision is made to offer these services.

"We encourage authors to understand the challenges for a Christian bookstore," said Smith. "Know what the challenges are and help us create an expanded customer base. Just like authors want their books discovered, we want our stores discovered."

••• Visit bakerbookstore.com •••

## Where Is Christian Retail Going?

"I don't believe Christian retail is collapsing, but I do think we need to re-align how we do business," said Sue Smith, manager of Baker Book House in Grand Rapids, Michigan. "The best stores will survive because there are a lot of people out there who know what they're doing."

Online presence is an absolute must, with a store's online space as much a gathering place as the brick-and-mortar store. Offer customers an easy way to buy books and other products online when they can't get to the store.

"There's a hard tension between doing business and doing ministry," said Smith. "There's been a much greater emphasis on how we do ministry and smaller emphasis on how to do business well. We need to merge those better."

Christian retail is at a point of no return when it comes to an online presence. It must be there, she said, pointing to the huge increase of online buying around the holidays.

"Christian retail is a place the church at large can gather to experience community and different forms of Christian thought," said Smith. "It's a place people can come to and feel safe."

## Assignments

1. What is your relationship with Christian retail? Do you have a store in your area? Do you shop there? Direct your readers to Christian retail? Make a list of how you might better use the assets of Christian retail in your writing and book promotion.

2. As an author, what can you bring to a Christian retailer to entice them to do an event with you? Describe how your platform can help them.

3. Research the three Christian bookstores closest to you to find out the kinds of events they do, who you can contact, and the online presence they have. What about general market bookstores? Do the same thing.

4. Create a bookstore event plan for your book. List the things you can offer the bookstore such as pushing the event on your social media, how many people you can bring in (be realistic), and tangibles such as providing light snacks. List the things they can do for you. Present this to your local Christian retailer.

5. Look at your social media to find out where you are directing readers to buy your book. How can you better direct them to Christian retail? Make changes as needed.

# Cultivating Your Audience: Publicity Advice from an Expert

## 37

KAREN CAMPBELL

Karen Campbell has gotten author clients on the *Today* show, on nationally syndicated radio programs, in magazines and newspapers. She's traveled the country with her authors, hobnobbing in New York City and Los Angeles and spots in between.

Those successes come from a combination of knowing the media outlets, building relationships with them, and knowing the books and authors she works with.

"I assess every book that comes my way and put together a publicity plan tailored to that book based on the media I've worked with in the past 20 years," said Campbell, owner of Karen Campbell Media.

She began her career with houses such as Baker Publishing Group and Zondervan, but has been a freelance publicist for the last several years. Ninety percent of her work comes from publishers who contract her services; the remaining comes from authors who hire her.

"There are a lot of roles that come with being a publicist. I can be a psychiatrist, counselor, and best friend. I create media lists, pitch to media, send books out, write press materials. And I go along to be the author's support system if she is booked on a big national program," she said. "I make sure the author gets where he or she needs to go."

Campbell has worked with shy authors and demanding ones. Those experienced at public speaking, those who aren't. Authors whose books are immediately snapped up by the media, those whose aren't. She's celebrated with authors and talked a few of them away from the cliff's edge of despair. She has seen it all and done it all when it comes to media.

There are three main things that make up a successful relationship between author and publicist: availability, communication, and expectations.

"Availability always comes up in initial conversations with an author," Campbell said. "Will an author be able to talk to me during the work day or do interviews during the work day? Will an author return my emails in a timely manner?"

If she gets a hit on the *Today* show or a nationally syndicated radio show, she needs to know immediately if the author is available during the time slots the show offers. Authors can't wait two or three days to respond because those slots will be taken by others and she'll need to start over.

It's also important for Campbell (and any publicist) to know when an author will be on vacation and therefore unavailable and about speaking engagements where they might tie in media events such as radio programs or book signings. Which is where communication comes in. "I'm a 'more communication is better' person," said Campbell.

Authors should let publicists know about speaking events, media connections they have, other writers they're connected with. "If an author is serious about promoting his or her book, every little bit helps. We can celebrate the small things and the big things, but it all adds to the snowball effect for the book in the end," she said.

Another key topic to address is expectations. "If I sense an author is going into the project with really high expectations—and it's okay to have high expectations—there has to be a reality check," she said.

The book is that author's baby, so it's hard to see that everyone isn't the audience. But it's a specific audience that Campbell and other publicists target with their media pitches. Also, authors may get lots of interviews but book sales don't follow. A publicist can't make potential readers buy the book and can't make a television or radio program, a newspaper, or online media accept the pitch.

"If an author doesn't hear from the publicist, the author thinks they aren't doing anything. But they're just not getting nibbles," said Campbell, who sends weekly updates to her publicity clients.

She also touts the benefit of local media large and small in an author's home area.

"I always go to the local media. Authors love it because friends and family see it, it makes them feel special, and they might sell books," said Campbell. "But it's also sharable on the author's social media and his or her friends' social media."

Social media is a must, she said. "You cannot be an author and not have an online presence, whether through a website, Instagram, Facebook, or the latest social media tool," she said. "The bigger the audience the better, but an author at least needs to be on social media simply because so many readers get recommendations from online sources."

Readers get a recommendation through an online contact or friend; one of the first things they do is look for that author or his or her book online. An online search should at least reveal a Facebook page to visit, or a website, blog, Twitter, Instagram, or other online space.

Campbell also urges cultivating a good relationship with your in-house or outside publicist. Your publicist will work for you for sure, but a demanding and complaining author makes it that much harder in an already tough media environment.

"Authors tend to love their editors because they make the book better and they love the sales people because they sell books, but authors can feel like the publicists and marketers are never doing enough," she said. "It's a different relationship, but my advice is to be friends with the publicity person."

Publicity expert Campbell offers a quick list of her best advice:

1. Nail down who the book's audience is and be specific.

2. List your dream media outlets or ones that could benefit the book, and the ones you have connections with.

3. Really think about that one hook that will sell your book to the producer of a local or national media outlet.

4. Develop good relationships with the marketing and publicity teams.

5. Be realistic about expectations.

6. Continue to cultivate your current audience, but don't stop trying to get more readers.

7. Make and keep personal connections with established authors.

8. At speaking engagements, take time for a one-on-one conversation with the person getting a book signed.

"Keep in touch with your audience; make personal connections," said Campbell. "Some of the most successful authors I've worked with have gotten to know their audience on a personal level. Always actively try to gain new readers, but don't ignore your fan base because you need them to get those new readers."

••• Visit karencampbellmedia.com •••

---

### Publicity vs. Marketing

**Publicity**—Getting exposure for your book through editorial content such as book reviews, print and live interviews, and excerpts that do not cost marketing dollars.

**Marketing**—Promoting your book through means that cost money such as paid advertisements, sending books to predetermined bloggers, and guest blog spots.

## Assignments

1.  What is your book's one main hook and how will that hook appeal to the media? Write it down.

2.  Make a list of media people you know personally or media outlets you have connections with such as hometown television and radio stations and print/online media, and national media.

3.  What are your expectations for your publicist and for yourself? Make a list and be realistic (no, you probably won't get on *The View* or *Entertainment Tonight*).

4.  How are you cultivating your audience? What else can you do?

5.  How might you build a good relationship with your publicist, or how can you repair that relationship now?

# Using Your Tribe: Leveraging Platform to Promote Nonfiction Books

## 38

ROBIN BARNETT

Robin Barnett has seen some great book proposals in her role as nonfiction publicity manager at Zondervan. She's also voted to turn down a fair number of those projects because authors hadn't yet developed a strong reach into his or her readership base. Reaching potential readers with information about the book (and author) is just as important as a great idea, great writing, and a great cover.

"Publishing is risky so we need to see that the author has a way to reach readers early on," said Barnett. "We look for authors with a tribe that is strong and loyal."

She and her team aren't looking only for authors who are super active on all social media and have a popular newsletter, blog, website, and podcast. They're looking for authors who reach readers best where and how they can.

"We want you to find where you flourish and can be real, and focus on that," said Barnett.

Barnett is quick to point out that your social media shouldn't be all about your book or books, though the subject matter should likely point in the general direction of the book. For example, an author writing a parenting book but whose entire social media points toward gardening may want to tweak his or her social media. That same author can be talking about parenting issues on social media, but not have every post point toward the book.

"There's a time to do hard sell, but social media is mostly about being a real person and not being annoying," said Barnett. "But if you find, as you're writing, that you're *not* talking about the topic of your book but about something else that excites you, it might be time to rethink what your book is about."

The bottom line is that authors who are shopping a book or who already have a book published need to find a way to interact on social media about topics or in ways that parallel the book.

## Contract in Hand

Once you have a contract in hand, publishers can help with an author's reach into his or her readership. The editorial and publicity teams can help you craft your messages and refine the topics you address on your blog and other social media.

"The key is staying consistent on social media," said Barnett. "And being open to feedback from publishers. When publishers suggest something, know it's not a personal attack but instead a publisher wanting to make the book and social media messages the best they can be."

She also suggests that authors contribute to media outlets that are talking about the topic of the book. So if your book is on parenting a special needs child, begin reading and commenting on blogs that speak to that topic and join Facebook groups on the topic.

"Those things are reaching the same readers you want to reach," Barnett said. "You want that audience to begin to know your name."

She recommends writing for websites or guest blogging on the topic of your book, again to reach those similar readers. Be willing to give away a bit of content for free, but prioritize building your platform versus spending time writing for others' social media. Focus on your own social media first and write for others in the time you have left.

Building an email list is also important. If you have a website, offer readers the option to receive your newsletter or blog sent right to their email. Have sign-ups at your speaking events; offer a giveaway on your blog and gather those emails.

Why an email list? These are folks who have taken an active step—signing up online or in person—to hear from you and, therefore, may be more likely to purchase your book. It's one thing to read a blog; it's completely another to click a few more times to begin receiving an email newsletter or information about new blog posts.

Barnett has advice for those writing memoir, a genre resurging these days. She cautions authors to be careful about giving away too much of your story on social media. If you do, your story is used up before the book releases. Readers will have no reason to buy the book if you've already revealed all the secrets in it.

## Expectations

Once you have a contract and your nonfiction book is scheduled, you can expect several things from the publisher and publicist.

*Querying media outlets.* Publicists will query media outlets, using their contacts to try to place you on television, radio, podcasts, print and online magazines, and newspapers.

"Authors need to see the publicity team as the experts; they know what they're doing and know how to bring your book to the correct media outlets," said Barnett. "But we have influence; we don't have control of those outlets."

*Communication.* Publicists will call and/or email to touch base and let you know about media requests. They expect you to respond quickly to their requests because media outlets fill slots quickly, particularly radio programs. If you wait three days to respond, that slot is gone and you've missed an opportunity.

She also urges authors to keep track of their media schedules. Mistakes happen and sometimes interviews are missed. Once can be understandable, but if a pattern of missing scheduled media opportunities persists, your publicist simply won't schedule any more of them.

Publicists are eager to hear an author's suggestions on media opportunities and pitch angles—within reason of course. If you have a solid connection to Oprah, by all means share it. If your brother-in-law hosts a popular radio show that fits your audience, please pursue it or pass along the contact information to your publicist.

"Authors have brought us suggestions about where a book would fit, and it was something we hadn't heard of," said Barnett. "Your publicist isn't an expert on everything you're an expert on."

Just make sure to let your publicist know who you're contacting so you're not duplicating efforts, especially regarding local media. Authors know their hometown media outlets better than the publicist may. Either send contact information to your publicist or contact local media yourself.

Publicists and publicity teams have expectations too. They expect you to respond to emails, keep track of your publicity events, and help with media connections. Barnett offered several other suggestions.

1. Don't be a jerk to your publicist. If you have issues, talk to your agent before sending fiery emails when you're angry. (Your agent will have schooled you on this anyway; listen to your agent!) If you have concerns, express them constructively.

2. Don't set your expectations too high. Publicists can't make a media outlet schedule you, can't make sure all reviews are positive, can't guarantee that you'll have 50 interviews in the week your book comes out.

3. Don't be encouraged or discouraged if your publisher hires an outside publicity firm. "Don't judge success or failure based on whether an outside firm is hired," said Barnett.

4. Don't focus on the negatives. Barnett and her team encourage authors to focus on the good things—radio or print interviews, reviews, speaking requests—instead of focusing on the fact that you didn't get on the *Today* show.

5. Have access to a landline for some interviews. Certain media, especially radio, need authors to use a landline to avoid dropped calls and other issues. Find a friend or perhaps your church that still uses a landline for those interviews.

Your publicist is one member of your publishing team, all of whom want your book to succeed. You are a member of that team as well; learning to work with your teammates makes success that much more possible.

"Expect a partner who wants you to succeed, who wants you to find your readers," said Barnett. "For a first-time author, you'll do a lot of work but you'll have people helping you. We want you to succeed; we want to build a long-term relationship. We look for people we think are going places."

••• Visit zondervan.com •••

## Assignments

1. Build an influencer list—those people you know who can help you get the word out about your book. This can include author friends who can mention your book on their social media, to connections in local media, public figures, and others. The list should include for each influencer their name, title, website, email, phone number, and pertinent details.

2. Think through how you feel about promoting your book. Sometimes authors are squeamish about talking about their book—"I don't want to be prideful!"—but there are ways to do so without being annoying. How do you feel about promotion? What can you do? Who can you talk to for advice?

3. Practice answering interview questions. Learn to stay on topic, avoid "ums," "like," and other fillers, and be succinct. Consider taking a course in public speaking, finding podcasts or blogs on the topic, or reading books such as *An Essential Guide to Public Speaking: Serving Your Audience with Faith, Skill, and Virtue* by Quentin Schultze.

4. Make a list of the things you expect from your publicist. Talk to your agent or a published author to see if you're being realistic. Amend the list as needed.

5. Scour the Internet to find websites, podcasts, and blogs that address topics similar to your book. If appropriate, begin commenting and participating in those venues. Where might you guest blog? Write an article? Begin making a list.

# Meeting Your Readers: Using Platform to Promote Your Novel

# 39

AMY GREEN

Novelists face unique challenges when it comes to building a platform that points readers to their books. There isn't a built-in and obvious topic like nonfiction writers have; readers searching for books on a specific topic aren't usually looking for novels to meet their needs. What is a novelist to do?

Publicist Amy Green, who has been with fiction powerhouse Bethany House for half a dozen years, offers advice to novelists looking to jump on the social media bandwagon. Her first piece of advice is to write a great book.

"Your writing is your strongest marketing tool," she said. "You won't sell books without having a well-written book."

There are thousands of people writing good books and many are getting very good at the craft, said Green, but fewer are out there connecting with readers in a well-thought-out, careful way. She suggests finding your niche audience tied to your books and connecting with them.

Kristi Ann Hunter is writing Regency novels, and has an active blog offering fun facts about the Regency era. Other examples include Jennifer Lamont Leo's Sparking Vintage Fiction blog that points to her Roaring Twenties novels, and Sarah Sundin's website featuring all kinds of information on WWII, the setting for her novels (see chapter 24).

Other novelists such as Tamera Alexander, Colleen Coble, and Denise Hunter provide readers with information about themselves and their books.

"Authors are worried about how they can get an audience; we're looking at how authors will use social media once they have a book published," said Green. "We're looking at the ability to market the book to fiction readers once it's out."

She's also looking for authors who know how the publishing industry works and are involved in writing communities such as American Christian Fiction Writers and Romance Writers of America.

"This shows you have connections in the writing community, are learning the craft, and understand how the industry works," said Green. "I can always tell the difference between writers who have been to conferences and are learning the process, and those who just throw a proposal at Bethany."

She suggests that would-be fiction authors (and even published novelists) ramp up the marketing sections of their proposals—making sure it's all true, of course—by including the following:

1. A well-written synopsis. "It's important for us to know where the story is going, to get a clear understanding of the big picture," said Green. "We need the themes and where the major characters are going." This is the place to tell, not show, the story from beginning to end.

2. Well-defined audience. Specify your target audience, defining the readers you'll reach such as those who liked *Downton Abbey* or who love biblical fiction. "Know who you're aiming at," said Green.

3. Comparable titles. List three to five books similar in theme, historical setting, or amount of humor. Include similarities and differences, general (secular) market titles if appropriate, with most published within the last five years. "We want to hear about any similarities that say 'my book will also sell to people who liked these books,'" she said.

4. Marketing/publicity strategy. This section should include local media contacts, alumni magazines, your own social media numbers, writers groups and organizations you belong to, endorsements if you have them (many debut authors don't), contest wins, newsletter numbers, and your website.

5. Word count. Publishers want to know you're writing within their specifications which are, typically, 80–90,000 words for contemporary novels; up to 100,000 for historical; 120–130,000 for fantasy.

6. Optionals: two-paragraph synopses of other books in a potential series; e-book novella ideas; preorder campaign ideas.

"Don't overstate what your book can do," said Green. "There's a difference between saying your story will appeal to Debbie Macomber fans and saying everyone thinks you're a better writer that Macomber. And don't say God directly inspired the story and you wrote it just as he told you to."

All that said, Green still focuses on the writing. She's read proposals from authors who have a wonderful audience and potential movie deals already in the works, but she's not sold on the writing.

"The writing still needs to be highest quality. Don't depend on a great marketing plan to compensate for mediocre sample chapters," said Green.

Once you have a contract for your novel, certain protocols exist for what the publicist expects from you and what you can expect from your publishing team.

1. Good communication. Green said that authors are good at communicating with the editor working on the book but not always with the marketing/publicity team. She encourages authors to let the publicist know what you're doing to promote the book including library visits, book clubs, speaking events, and local media.

"Before the book releases, have a discussion with the marketing team to find out what is expected as far as when to communicate and what is too much. Ask meaningful questions," she said.

2. Avoid bad communication, such as demands for them to do things for you, fretting about publicity opportunities (there aren't as many for novelists as nonfiction authors), and fussing over design issues.

"Let the designers design," she said. "If you don't think the book cover is great, talk about it. But don't nitpick. Make sure your complaints are legitimate. It never hurts to politely discuss things, but when it's small stuff like bookmarks, posters, and brochures, let it go. Know that the designers are experts."

3. Be sure to give lots of advance notice if you need posters, bookmarks, brochures, or other materials. Those things need to be written, designed, and printed, so the more advance notice the better.

4. Check your email at least once a day and let your publicist know when you'll be on vacation and/or can't respond. When your publicist asks about media opportunities, she needs a quick response lest the opportunities be lost.

5. Have at least one self-owned media such as a blog, website, or newsletter so readers can find you consistently, and find one social media platform where your readers go that you also are part of. This is often Facebook but can be other platforms as well.

There are several big no-nos when it comes to social media and publicity.

First is turning your social media into a platform for political rants or theological arguments. Posting some personal stuff is fine—think pet pictures or your latest knitting project—but if you say something controversial there needs to be a very good reason for doing so such as your book is tied to that controversy in some way.

Second is ignoring other authors. Green encourages novelists to help promote each other, to be generous to each other regarding social media. Invite other authors to guest blog for you, be willing to mention their books and guest blog for them.

"Writers promoting each other is very helpful," she said. "Authors eager to promote other authors are easier to work with."

Finally, don't be a diva. Divas make demands instead of asking questions and are difficult to work with instead of eager to work as a team.

"We've had publishing board meetings at which we discuss renewing contracts with authors. One of the deciding factors is how easy the author is to work with," said Green.

Green, who often attends writers conferences, addresses several questions that come up repeatedly:

Q: Should I write the book I want to write or write to the market?

A: Approach this question with balance. Green and her team can always tell when someone is writing to the trends in the market. Some authors have set aside a book or series that is difficult to sell in favor of one easier to sell, then bring out the other later.

---

## Advice from a Publicity Expert – Katie Schroder Hall

"Authors can't underestimate the importance of networking. It's the secret sauce that separates fiction authors who are successful in launching their first books and those who aren't," said Katie Schroder Hall, a marketing and publicity expert.

Schroder Hall spent eight years as head of marketing and publicity for Harper Collins Christian Publishing's fiction lines, and before that worked for WaterBrook and Zondervan. She has seen the publishing landscape for Christian fiction change dramatically in recent years.

Now readers expect an author to be present and available online. Readers ask a question on the author's social media and expect a response; most of the time they get one.

One of best things a fiction author can do is connect online with your peer group—writers on the same journey you are—and connect with writers ahead of you on the publishing process.

Schroder Hall has seen authors make mistakes when it comes to their writing careers. First is the posture a writer takes with readers. "Authors I've seen succeed most consistently are humble. There isn't an expectation of success; these authors are grateful when readers read and comment on their books. There really is an endearing humbleness," she said. "Which can be worked on if it doesn't come naturally."

The other mistake is to stop creating content. Novelists should be constantly writing the next story and learning the pace of life required to deliver content on a regular basis, whether new novels or novellas, blog posts, newsletters, or social media posts.

"There should never be a sense of 'I have arrived because I have a contract.' Authors should be asking questions about what they can change and improve to build a career," said Schroder Hall.

Q: Can I switch genres after writing several books?

> A: The sales team says to stay in your genre because it's easier to place on the shelves, but some authors have done it well, especially earlier in a career. You can always stick within your brand, such as a humorous tone or specific themes.

••• Visit bethanyhouse.com •••

## Assignments

1.  Assess your social media. How are you reaching your potential readers? Are you appealing to a specific group of readers tied to the topic or genre of your book?

2.  Visit your favorite novelists' websites, blogs, and other social media. What makes you feel welcome or turns you off? How might you incorporate some of those ideas in your own social media?

3.  Think about your communication style. Do you demand or discuss? Create questions for your publicist to help you prepare for future discussions.

4.  When have you turned your social media platform into a political or theological forum? How did that work out? What was the response?

5.  Make a list of the topics or areas you might focus on that reflect the topics or genre of your novel. Now look for websites or blogs that you might connect with, comment on, or guest blog.

# The Business of Writing

# Publishing Options: Choosing the Best Method to Get Your Book into the World

**40**

TIM BEALS

### Dr. Carol's Story

Tim Beals, founder and publisher of Credo House Publishers, shares the publishing success story of one of his authors, Carol Peters-Tanksley, MD, DMin. Dr. Carol, as she's called by many, approached Credo House with nearly a dozen book ideas.

"We considered her carefully because she had an excellent background," he said. "A medical degree, a master's and doctorate in theology, completed proposals and samples for three different books, a large platform online through her blog, Twitter, and Facebook, and she was host of a Sirius XM call-in radio show on the Doctor Radio channel."

However, she had one major liability. She was unpublished.

Through Credo House she was able to custom publish her first manuscript and later publish her next two books with traditional publisher Charisma House (see chapter 5).

"Her story is one that we see repeated by authors over and over. Choosing a publishing method is no longer a matter of 'either/or' but 'both/and,'" he said.

In today's publishing world, the new normal is that authors can custom publish some books and have others published traditionally without limiting themselves to one or the other.

### Three Publishing Options

Beals explained that authors have three main options for publication: traditional or legacy publishing; self-publishing (also called DIY publishing); and custom or partnership publishing.

**Traditional publishing** is what most people know best. Houses such as Zondervan, Charisma House, and InterVarsity Press are traditional publishers. Small and large traditional houses offer royalties and advances.

The benefits of traditional publishing are the expert personnel behind the book (including editors and marketers), the decreased personal risk (since the publisher takes on the cost of development), and established promotional and distribution networks.

There are also drawbacks to this method. Statistically only 1 to 2 percent of authors get published this way. They have less control over the message and presentation of the book once they agree to be published by a traditional house. These books are notoriously slow to market, taking anywhere between one and two years from contract to finished book. Finally, there is little financial reward with a traditional publishing house, often much less than with other publishing methods. If you plan to publish traditionally, "don't quit your day job," Beals advises.

The second option is **self-publishing**, the opposite of traditional publishing in that it involves doing all the work yourself—editing, page layout, cover design, marketing, publicity, and sales. Those who choose self-publishing typically use online outlets such as CreateSpace, Lulu, and AuthorHouse. This method has several benefits, including complete creative control, 100 percent profit from book sales, speed to market—usually one or two days—and low cost of entry (around $500–$1,500).

As Beals points out, "Self-published books are sometimes lower quality and there may be no financial return from your efforts and money" if sales are low. Self-publishing requires more risk by the author, especially financially.

**Custom or partnership publishing** is a third option. The benefits of custom publishing include working with an expert on your book; quick turnaround time into the marketplace, with work on the book usually lasting two to six weeks; a large financial incentive with the author keeping 100 percent of the profit; and assistance with distribution, marketing, and cross-promotion.

The drawback of this publishing method is the cost of entry, which starts around $2,000 and ranges upward to $10,000 or more, depending on the length and complexity of the manuscript. Examples include Credo House Publishers, Redemption Press, and EA Books Publishing.

### A Quick Look at the Numbers

Beals emphasizes the importance of evaluating traditional and custom publishing by understanding your goals and comparing the numbers.

Let's say you publish 1,000 books through both traditional publishing and custom publishing; take a look at the numbers:

- 1,000 books sold at $20 each through custom publishing = $20,000 in gross proceeds. Take away $5,000 for the cost of goods sold (developing and printing the books) and that's $15,000 in net proceeds *the author can keep.*

- For a traditionally published book, gross proceeds are $10,000 for the same 1,000 books sold (bookstores typically buy books at a 50 percent discount and then sell the book to their customers for the original sticker price). The author receives a 15 percent royalty rate on this $10,000, bringing the total profit for the author down to $1,500 (the rest goes to the publisher). Then the author must subtract 15 percent for the agent fee (the split is 85 percent/15 percent between author and agent, respectively). Although the author spent nothing, this leaves the author with *only $1,275 in net proceeds.* To make the same $15,000 from traditional publishing, the publisher would have to sell *12,000 more books.*

Potential self-publishing and custom publishing authors should also remember they must do the marketing, publicity, and sales on their own. Setting up radio, television, and print interviews can be difficult without connections, and getting reviews in major outlets is difficult. However, self- or custom publishing can be a great option if the author has ways to sell books already in place, such as an active speaking ministry or online presence.

### The Moral of the Story

Using custom or self-publishing allows authors to make more money, get their book into the marketplace immediately, and actually know they will get published. Beals has consistently seen authors who chose this option make ten times more than traditionally published authors *with the same amount of effort.* Instead of waiting years for your book to get into the marketplace, custom and self-publishing allows this to happen in just days or weeks.

"We have to remember the 'narrow gate.' Very few people get published by traditional publishing houses when they are previously unpublished. But getting published through custom and self-publishing is a guarantee," he said.

Choosing custom publishing doesn't limit your future options with traditional publishers either, and it may expand your options for later publishing pursuits, according to Beals. Think "both/and" not "either/or."

••• Visit credohousepublishers.com •••

### Assignments

1.  Think through your publishing goals, then make a list of them. Which type of publishing seems to match those goals best? Why?

2.  Talk with writers who have published in each of these ways. Ask them the pros and cons of each, and what they might do differently next time.

3.  Create a list of custom and traditional publishing houses that are options for you. Consider costs and financial gains of each. Consider how customers rate these houses.

4.  Choose the top three that would match your goals well. What sorts of books do they publish and what do they look for? Describe how your book would fit there. While it may not be required, consider developing a complete book proposal for your project.

5.  If you are considering custom and self-publishing, research strategies to sell your book. There are many helpful resources online.

# Going Indie: Pros, Cons, and the Scoop on Publishing Yourself

## 41

HEATHER DAY GILBERT

Heather Day Gilbert's publishing story is like so many others—a fair number of rejections, a revolving door of agents, and a depressingly long time between book idea and publication, should she ever get a contract. She decided to consider other paths toward publication, focusing on independent publishing, specifically self-publishing.

Gilbert knew that Viking tales were trending in the general market and she just happened to have a Viking novel needing a home. One Christian publisher was interested, but didn't know how they would market such a novel. Others wanted to change the setting of the tale.

Instead of waiting even longer or changing her book completely, she decided to self-publish *God's Daughter*, book one in the Vikings of the New World Saga. The book released in 2013 through CreateSpace, with the second in the series, *Forest Child*, out in October 2016.

Amid Gilbert's decision to indie publish—conquering the learning curve and marketing the books—she also wrote and indie published *Miranda Warning* and *Trial by Twelve*, books one and two in A Murder in the Mountains series, and *Out of Circulation*, volume one in the Hemlock Creek Suspense series. She now has seven indie-published books out.

"My best advice is to not rush into indie publishing," said Gilbert. "Authors expect to sell a lot of books, but it's an uphill climb with so many indie books out there. And you have to compete with or be better than traditionally published books."

She calls her experience as a self-published author "mostly all positive," listing several advantages:

- Working on your own schedule, creating and releasing the book when it and you are ready

- Jumping genres, which traditional publishers usually don't recommend. Gilbert has released Viking historicals, contemporary mysteries, and nonfiction. "I have readers for both fiction series; some readers overlap but many don't," she said.

- Controlling your own pricing, which she deems "huge." Gilbert can run a sale on her Viking novels on Leif Erikson Day or offer discounts on the mysteries on Sherlock Holmes' birthday.

    When the second in her A Murder in the Mountains series released, she offered the first one for free across all platforms. She actually saw an increase in sales of both books because of the pricing incentive.

    Side note: Don't offer the first book in a series for free unless you have a second book already out there.

- Marketing flexibility. You can place ads—think Facebook, Google, Amazon, websites, occasionally print—when and where you want and tie the ads to sale prices you set. You can also keep your ebook prices the same, not reducing prices after the book has been out awhile, which traditional publishers often do on ebooks.

    "With traditional publishing, there's usually a big launch push for a month or so, then it's sink or swim," she said. When you're in charge of the marketing, you can decide when, where, and how much to promote.

## Cost and Pricing

Self-publishing can be as inexpensive as a couple hundred dollars—Gilbert's first book cost her under $300—or into the thousands depending on editing and cover costs. Now that she's made a little money, Gilbert spends about $300 on a cover alone because she's learned the importance of a great one.

You'll probably pay between $250 and $800 for a cover designed by a pro. Stand-alone premade covers are available for around $80 (search "premade book covers"), and websites such as Damonza offer stock covers.

"The minute you show readers your cover, you want them to say 'Wow!'," she said. "And if you're planning a series, choose a cover that can be branded."

Along with a great cover, indie authors must have a quality book unburdened by typos, bad grammar, and subpar writing. She encourages authors to pay an editor and a proofreader (they aren't the same) to clean up the manuscript.

"Most authors should pay for an editor unless they have a lot of good beta readers," she said. "You want to put your best foot forward from the very first book. That sets the bar high for your readers, and it's better to do it right the first time."

Other things you may spend money on: bookmarks, business cards, newsletters, ads, a website. Gilbert said you don't need to purchase these right away, and suggests that you don't need a top-of-the-line website right away. She also suggests bartering for services to cut costs.

"I think you can produce a good book for under $500 if you have people in place who can help," said Gilbert.

Gilbert—as do most indie authors—makes the majority of her income from ebook sales. She started out on the Amazon platform only, but as she has gained experience she has added iBooks, Nook, and Kobo, with trade paperbacks available through CBD and print-on-demand. Softcovers are also available online through Walmart, Books-a-Million and others.

Study the indie market, talk to other indie authors, read up on the topic and research your pricing model, Gilbert recommends.

"Indie publishing is a huge learning process," she said. "The model is constantly changing so authors need to be constantly learning. If you want to self-publish, you have to have a long-term plan."

In the Christian publishing world, professionals used to talk down about indie-published books, but "the game has changed, and Christian indie authors have set the bar high. Christian indies are standouts in the field and have gotten awards outside of Christian circles," she said.

Gilbert has received a starred review in *Publishers Weekly* for *Forest Child*, and a Grace Award for *Trial by Twelve*. She's also now a traditionally published author thanks to a contract with Barbour Publishing for her part in the story collection *Message in a Bottle.*

Gilbert has codified her knowledge in *Indie Publishing Handbook: Four Key Elements for the Self-Publisher*, which she indie published, of course.

"I know indie publishing was the right decision for me," she said. "Indie authors can definitely make an income; many traditionally published authors will eventually also indie publish some of their books."

••• Visit heatherdaygilbert.com •••

## Four Elements of Indie Publishing

The very definition of indie publishing is that you are in charge of all aspects of your book's publication . . . from cover art to formatting, from edits to uploading. In fact, I would say there are **four** key elements indie authors control when publishing their books. By control, I mean you are the overseer—you can outsource it or learn to do it yourself. But the goal is to bring a competitive book to your readers, so you want to use the best you can afford or learn to be the best in these four aspects.

The four elements are as follows:
- Editing
- Cover art / book blurb
- Formatting / uploading
- Marketing

Heather Day Gilbert, *Indie Publishing Handbook* (CreateSpace, 2017), 5.

## Assignments

1. Reread chapter 40 to familiarize yourself with the publishing options available. Focus on indie (independent/self) publishing. List the pros and cons for your specific book, based on that chapter and this one.

2. Look over the four elements listed above. Which one will be the steepest learning curve for you? Why?

3. Create a list of people or websites you can tap into for help with editing, cover design, and formatting/uploading. How might you barter for services?

4. What is the marketing plan for your book? Do you have social media already in place? A blog? What resources might you tap into to get the word out about your book?

5. Study ebook pricing and set up a short-term and long-term pricing plan, including sale prices and events.

# Book Proposals: Whys and Hows of Creating a Great Overview of Your Book

**42**

ANN BYLE

Several chapters in *Christian Publishing 101* address aspects of writing a great book proposal. Lorilee Craker included excellent advice in her chapter "Sell the Sizzle." Amy Green talked about what to include in the marketing section of a fiction book proposal in her chapter. This chapter offers more detailed information on the ingredients of an excellent book proposal, with genre-specific information as well.

Each book proposal is different because each writer is different. Your proposal will reflect your heart, your personality, and your unique voice. That said, don't go wild on fancy fonts, goofy layout, and lots of graphics. Go with Times New Roman font or similar, 12-point type, double spaced, and 1-inch margins.

The book proposal is a professional document that is a publisher's introduction to you, a document to be perused by editorial, sales, and marketing people, and a clear and concise summarization of your book.

**Title Page:** Center the book title, subtitle, and author's name. In the lower left corner list author's name and contact information, or the agent's name and contact information.

**One-Sentence Overview:** Summarize your book in one sentence; be concrete and concise.

Good: *Christian Publishing 101* offers readers concrete information on all aspects of Christian publishing via interviews with authors and publishing professionals.

Needs work: *Christian Publishing 101* will help you get your book published thanks to help from many people.

**Synopsis:** One or two paragraphs that deepen the one-sentence overview. For nonfiction, it deepens details on issues the book addresses, felt needs it meets, the author's authority, and lists features such as in-depth interviews and study questions. For a novel, the synopsis adds details about setting, characters, theme, and plot.

**Detailed Synopsis** (fiction only): You may want to include a detailed plot synopsis for your novel in the proposal. This should be no more than two pages (double spaced) and offer more depth and details than your shorter synopsis.

**About the Author:** Include relevant details such as education, job experience, previous publications, life experience, where you live and a little about your family (if desired). No need to include your complete resume or list of academic publications (list the top few if you're writing to the academic market). Include a picture if desired. Write this in the third person, avoiding "I" and "me."

**BISAC Subject Heading:** BISAC is the acronym for Book Industry Standards and Communications; it's an industry-approved list of subject descriptors used in the transfer of information, in bibliographies, and as shelving guides. For more information, visit bisg.org.

**Book Details:** Word count, manuscript completion date, format (trade paperback, hardcover, mass paperback, picture book, board book). Completion date can be "six months after contract" or "available immediately;" this is up to you, though don't say "two years after contract" because a publisher won't wait that long.

**Features and Benefits** (three to five of each): Think of features as nouns and benefits as verbs, with each feature having a corresponding benefit. For example, a feature of *Christian Publishing 101* is "interviews with authors and publishing professionals;" the benefit is "inside and in-depth information to help you understand the publishing process."

Another example: One feature of a children's book might be "simple explanations of biblical concepts such as love and faith." The benefit is "children can begin to see how God loves them and why they can trust him."

**Felt Need:** This section, one to two paragraphs long, addresses why this book is important to readers in the current cultural context. Can include statistics, cultural references, and studies. A book for women about body image can include information on recent studies or details about cosmetic surgeries in this country.

For *Christian Publishing 101*, we could include stats on how many people attend Christian writing conferences each year to highlight the need for "a writers conference in book form."

**Comparable Titles / Competitive Titles:** A list of books that compare to yours in some way, including tone, setting, theme, characterization. These should be published within the last five years, unless there is a classic that might be comparable. Be careful in comparing your book to a classic, though, because those books are classics for a reason.

Include book title and subtitle, author, publisher and release year; also

## Children's Book Proposals

Proposals for children's books need all of the elements listed here with the exception of a table of contents and chapter summaries (unless you're writing a children's reference book or YA nonfiction).

In the Book Details section, include details on grade, age, reading, and vocabulary levels, and whether it's a picture book, board book, or lift-the-flap format.

Proposals for children's books need the complete manuscript included.

Note on illustrations: Unless you are a professional illustrator, do not include illustrations with your complete manuscript. Publishers have professional designers and illustrators they use to create books that match their vision.

a one-sentence description of the book and a sentence or two about how yours compares and is different.

Example: *Redeeming Love* by Francine Rivers. Rivers' beloved novel retells the story of the biblical Hosea and Gomer, set during the Gold Rush of the 1850s. My novel, set in Victorian England, retells the biblical love story of Ruth and Boaz.

**Marketing and Publicity:** This section, which may be the largest in your proposal, details how you are reaching your readers now and plan to reach them before and as the book comes out. This section should include:

*Social media*: Your website, blog, Facebook, Instagram, Pinterest, and other social media. Include numbers such as Facebook followers and blog hits. Be specific.

*Email list*: Number of people who have signed up to receive your newsletter, or the number of people/emails you have accumulated. These are people who have gone the extra step to stay connected and may be good sources for book sales.

*Media contacts:* Specific media contacts you have including local radio/TV/print; friends with blogs, podcasts or radio programs who have promised to have you on; magazines you write for; media outlets that are a good fit for your book. Don't include Oprah, Jen Hatmaker, or Joel Osteen unless you actually know them.

*Endorsers/endorsements*: Include any endorsements you already have, plus a list of people you are in contact with or who might endorse your book. If you can, search out a few endorsements early to include in the proposal. See above regarding Oprah, Osteen, and Hatmaker.

*Speaking platform*: Include how often you speak, what kind of events, and how many attend. Publishers want to know how many books you can sell at the back of the room at your speaking events.

**Table of Contents:** Novel proposals don't need a table of contents, but a nonfiction proposal should include one.

**Chapter Summaries:** Chapter summaries for a nonfiction book can become the table of contents if desired; summaries should be one paragraph long and include relevant details such as topics covered or experts quoted. Publishers know that chapters can change as you write the book.

**Sample Chapters:** Fiction and nonfiction proposals should include the first three sample chapters of the book. Novels, however, should be completed before submitting the proposal; publishers will want to read the complete book especially if you are a debut or early published author. Nonfiction books don't have to be complete to submit a proposal.

••• Visit annbylewriter.com •••

## Assignments

1. Create a one-sentence overview and a one- or two-paragraph synopsis of your book. How difficult or easy was this? How did this exercise help you define the essence of your book?

2. List three to five features and corresponding benefits of your book. Think of the features as nouns and the benefits as verbs. Be specific.

3. Research other books that compare to yours in theme, topic, time period (if a novel), and tone. List title, author, publisher/date, and what is similar and different about your book.

4. Research book proposals to see how your target editor or agent wants to receive them. How does yours compare?

5. Begin creating your marketing section including potential endorsers, social media numbers, and book launch plans. Research as needed. Where do you need work? What can you do now to begin beefing up this section?

## A Going Concern: Understanding the Legal and Business Side of Publishing

43

DREW CHAMBERLIN, JD

Writing is more than just typing words into a computer and sending them off in the hopes of publication. Any writer—whether sending out one poem a year or five queries a week—must handle the business side of writing at least once in a while. Magazine rights, copyrights, contracts, and literary agreements can be confusing. Drew Chamberlin, literary agent and intellectual property specialist at Credo Communications, deals with such things every day. He offers his expertise here.

### Copyright

To copyright a new literary, musical, or artistic work, the author must gain the exclusive, legally secured right to reproduce, publish, and/or sell the work. However, to get additional legal status (i.e., to get the right to sue and reclaim statutory damages and fees upon infringement) you should register with the U.S. Copyright Office. See copyright.gov for more information. Chamberlin points out that "just adding a copyright symbol and your name does not add valuable authority to your claim. You must register through the copyright office to attain that."

Everything you write does not need to be copyrighted, though books you self-publish should be. Traditional publishers will copyright in the author's name. Always seek legal consultation if you have questions.

### The "Four-Factor Balancing Test"

"Fair use" of copyrighted material is always a factor as you consider using copyrighted material from others in your own work, or if you are asked by other authors to use yours. Use the "four-factor balancing test" utilized by courts in such cases and consider the following questions.

1. *What is the purpose and character of your use of the material?* Does it transform the copied material in a meaningful way?

2. *What is the nature of the copyrighted work?* Is it published or unpublished? Factual or fictional?

3. *Consider the amount and substantiality of the portion taken.* How much of it have you used? How important is this portion to the copyrighted work?

4. *What effect could this use have on the (potential) market?* Does it diminish the commercial value of the copyrighted work in the marketplace?

If an author can't get through the four-factor test above with confidence that infringement (a violation of copyright laws) wouldn't take place, they shouldn't go any further.

Here's another tip: Never use song lyrics under any circumstances. Copyrights are tough, thorough, and carefully watched. Best to just stay away.

When in doubt about copyrighted material, he suggested that authors "play it safe and try to say it in your own words instead."

Work in the public domain—work that has never been copyrighted or the copyright has expired—is available to use. However, just because someone else's work hasn't been copyrighted doesn't give you the right to use it for yourself without attribution. No stealing!

## Literary Agreements

A literary agreement is a document that controls and explains the relationship between the author and the agent for as long as they are working together. This document (an LA) should be a win-win for both author and agent. Chamberlin added that it should not be an overly complicated document. "It should have clear responsibilities for both parties and an easy way out," he said. Key provisions found therein should include information about the financial arrangement and arbitration of the agreement should it be needed.

But beware! If any of the terms seem unclear or something about the agreement doesn't feel right, ask for clarification. You may want to consider legal counsel.

## Publisher Agreements or Contracts

A publisher agreement or contract controls the relationship between the author and the publishing house. There are a few key provisions that appear in these documents including advances and royalties, deadlines, and word count. Additional information includes rights, arbitration information, and cancellation of contract details, among other things. Again, Chamberlin encourages authors to seek legal counsel or ask for clarification if anything seems unclear or lopsided. An author's literary agent will act as intermediary between author and publisher, always looking out for the interests of the author.

## Attorneys

You may wonder if you need an attorney with experience in contracts or in intellectual property and entertainment law, especially if you have an agent. Chamberlin explains, "The answer is you may want to consider getting legal counsel if anything about the situation is unclear, if you want a clearer understanding of the document in question, or if you simply want additional peace of mind before moving forward."

Check out iael.org/members (International Association of Entertainment Lawyers) to find an attorney near you.

## Article Rights

Magazines or websites can purchase a variety of rights from you, the author. You are wise to consider what rights you want to give up to get a piece published.

All rights: Complete sale of your material; author has no further control of it and it cannot be used elsewhere.

First rights: Selling the right to publish a piece that hasn't been published before. Often a magazine or website will want first rights until the article is published.

One-time rights: Selling the right to publish a piece one time to a number of publications, usually in noncompeting markets

Reprint rights: Selling the right to reprint an article that has already been published; also called "second serial rights"

Books such as the *The Christian Writers Market Guide* (Christian Writers Institute, released annually) and the *Writer's Market* (Writer's Digest Books, released annually), plus any number of websites, offer advice and information on these topics.

••• Visit credocommunications.net/about-us/associates •••

## Assignments

1. Find sample book contracts online and read through them to get an idea of what they contain. Take notes on what confuses you.

2.  Study several magazines' writers guidelines to see what rights the magazine buys. How might you sell your work to these publications?

3.  Create a list of ways to avoid using copyrighted material. Remind yourself that there are always other options if you use your creativity.

4.  Check out copyright.gov and research the steps it takes to copyright your work. Ask an attorney or more experienced writers about copy-righting before circulating your work or if you are concerned about legality.

5.  Research several articles, websites, or books that talk about the legal issues related to a writing career. What questions do you have? Make a list of what you should do now to prepare for a writing career.

# Are You Ready? Approaching an Agent and Learning the Ropes

## 44

STEVE LAUBE

There's an old joke Steve Laube likes to tell about a writer who was on the table before brain surgery. The surgeon leans over the writer and asks what he does for a living.

"I'm a writer," said the patient.

"Oh, I'm going to write a book when I retire," replied the surgeon with surety.

"Well, when I retire from writing I'm going to be a brain surgeon," said the writer before he went under.

The joke is hilarious to experienced writers, editors, and agents who know that not just anybody can write a book, including Mensa-level brain surgeons.

Laube, a former bookseller and editorial director at Bethany House, has been a literary agent since 2003. As owner of The Steve Laube Agency, he has been approached by hundreds of authors seeking representation. He turns down most of them.

"The biggest mistake writers make is approaching me before they are ready," said Laube. "They haven't honed their craft, developed the idea, built a platform, and the proposal may be 80 percent ready. I'm not a book coach; I'm an agent. They are very different."

When he moved from bookseller to an editorial position at Bethany House, he took the time to learn how the industry worked. He studied and read and asked professionals with more experience. That love of learning still propels him today, causing him to read trade magazines such as *Publishers Weekly*, *Writers Digest*, *Christian Retailing*, *CBA Christian Market*, and a host of blogs.

"I appreciate any author, new or veteran, who is a student of the industry," he said. "It makes my job easier in that I don't have to explain everything, and but also helps the author anticipate what's happening in his or her specific market so they aren't taken by surprise."

Laube has learned through years of experience what to look for in a client and what makes good clients in general. Potential clients and veteran authors will find Laube's lists instructive.

**What Makes a Good Client**

1. Being willing to work hard

2. Meeting deadlines (agent and publisher)

3. Having a flexible spirit when it comes to editing

---

### How to Find a Literary Agent – Tim Beals

The hardest part of the entire process can be identifying the best agent for your work. But there is no shortcut. Do your research, starting with these resources:

- *Guide to Literary Agents* (Writer's Digest Books). A reference book published annually. Contains a comprehensive list of agents. Provides limited information on each agent.

- *Writers' Handbook* (JP&A Dyson). A reference book published annually. Includes a complete list of agents for the US market, plus separate entries for literary representatives in Canada, the UK, and Ireland.

- *Writer's Market* (Writer's Digest Books). A reference book published annually. Includes a much shorter list of agents, but each agent's interests, specialties, and credentials are described in detail.

- *Jeff Herman's Guide to Book Publishers, Editors and Literary Agents* (New World Library). A reference book published annually. Includes a comprehensive list of agents, including their interests, specialties, and experience—over 300 pages long!

- For an online list of top agents and agencies, visit the website of the Association of Authors' Representatives at aaronline.org.

Specialized Lists of Agents:

- *Children's Writer's and Illustrator's Market* (Writer's Digest Books). A reference book published annually. Contains a list of many agents who handle material for children and young adults. Each listing is very thorough.

---

4. Being entrepreneurial regarding marketing—willing to put yourself out there and to treat your writing as a small business

5. Seeing writing as your job or ministry

## What Makes a Bad Client

1. Being unresponsive to emails, calls, faxes, and any other form of communication

2. Chronically missing deadlines with poor excuses

3. Exploding verbally to publishing staff (editors, marketers, sales staff) without coming to the agent first

---

- *Christian Writers Market Guide* (Christian Writers Institute). A reference book published annually. Includes a chapter called "Literary Agents" with a list of agents and agencies representing Christian authors.

- *Dramatists Sourcebook* (Theatre Communications Group). A reference book now in its 26th edition. Includes many agents who handle material for the stage.

You are also encouraged to ask other people for information on agents they have worked with or know. Ask about agents' effectiveness, responsiveness, willingness to stick with a project, knowledge of the market, strengths, and weaknesses. People you might talk to include:

- Writers you know

- Editors and publishers with whom you have established a professional relationship (even if you've never sold them anything)

- Members, officers, and staff of any professional writers' organization to which you belong

- College professors of creative and professional writing. Many of these people have agents or knowledge of and experience with agents

- Faculty and organizers of writers' conferences and events.

---

Tim Beals, "Agenting 101: The What, Why, When, and Hows of Literary Representation" in *Jot That Down: Encouraging Essays for New Writers* ed. A.L. Rogers (Grand Rapids: Caffeinated Press, 2017), 116–117.

An agent's role is varied, ranging from taking care of business arrangements with publishers to helping an author through writer's block. A good agent plays all these roles at one time or another.

### An Agent's Job Description

1. Business manager
2. Teacher
3. Editor
4. Pastor
5. Mother
6. Drill sergeant
7. Career advisor
8. Rubber room (safe place to vent)
9. Problem solver
10. Advocate
11. Reality check
12. Negotiator

"I never want my clients to feel like I'm not responsive to them," he said. "I want them to feel like they're the only client I have. And I thank God for my job every day. I get to work in the world of ideas, where I can help writers in their efforts to change the world."

••• Visit stevelaube.com •••

### Assignments

1. Are you really ready to approach an agent? What do you need to do to get ready? Make a list and give yourself a reality check.

2. Give your book proposal a thorough edit, then ask a writing friend to look it over. If necessary, hire a professional to edit it.

3. Look over Laube's list of what makes a good client. Write out what each of these characteristics looks like in your writing life. What can you improve? Build on?

4. Read three articles about the craft of writing. Read one book. Make a list of things you'd like to know more about regarding the craft of writing or the life of a writer.

5. If you feel you're ready for an agent, research three agencies and its agent list to see who you might approach. Consider whether or not your work matches their interests, and follow the submission guidelines carefully.

# Managing Your Time: Making a Living as a Writer

## 45

JAMES SCOTT BELL

I know how busy you are. And I know you are interested in making a living as a writer.

We have to reconcile those two things.

That's why I've written this chapter on how to manage your time and your life. Some of this material I've mentioned in passing. Now I want to put it all together in a systematic way.

I'm going to give you these principles in the most efficient way I can. You are free to use them, adapt them, make them work for you. All with the goal of increasing your efficiency, productivity, and overall happiness.

Yes, happiness. I've discovered that the people who know what they're doing with time, which is after all our only real commodity, are the happiest people. They get the most done and are more likely to accomplish their goals.

While there are many courses out there on time management, which you could pay up to $500 or maybe even more to take, I just don't see the point. I'm going to give you everything you need to know about managing time and your life right here. (By the way, there's a great little book called *How to Get Control of Your Time and Your Life* by Alan Lakein. Pick up a used copy if you want to delve further into time management. *Time Power: A Proven System for Getting More Done in Less Time Than You Ever Thought Possible* by Brian Tracy is another excellent resource.)

Once you start practicing these methods, you'll be amazed at your increase in efficiency. It will almost be as if you are creating an extra hour in the day, and one that is productive to boot.

But first a couple of provisos.

This is not about becoming a military-style time nut. You have to have balance in life. What I'm giving you are only tools, and it's up to you to use them wisely.

I advocate taking time to loaf. Yes, schedule lazy time. For most of my life I've worked for myself, as a lawyer, entrepreneur, and writer. I have thus always been in charge of my own schedule. Early on I read something by Jay Conrad Levinson, the man who wrote the guerrilla series of books. In *The Way of the Guerrilla: Achieving Success and Balance as an Entrepreneur in the 21st Century*, Levinson extolled the value of taking Friday afternoons off. A simple suggestion, but one that I found I absolutely looked forward to. It made me work all the harder during the week just so I could loaf on Friday afternoon.

That's just an example of the flexibility you'll have when you know how to manage time.

First, I'm going to give you the 20 Power Tools for managing time. These will transform your life. Guaranteed.

Then I'll conclude with sections on how to handle problems and stress. Let's manage.

## The 20 Power Tools

### 1. Plan your weeks

The absolute number one rule of time management is you have to plan in advance. And the best way to plan is by the week.

I like to take some time on Sunday and look at the week ahead on the calendar. The first thing I do is mark every block of time where I have an obligation. These things could be work related, family related, whatever.

Once those are marked on the calendar, I'm free to start filling up the rest of the slots with prioritized tasks (see #2, below). This takes maybe five minutes to do, because I know already the tasks I need to perform.

### 2. Prioritize your tasks

Make a list of all the things you want and have to do, a master list of as many things as you can think of.

You're going to put these tasks into three different categories.

The first category is those tasks that you *must* do. You absolutely have to complete these things in order to accomplish your goals and do your work well.

Put an A next to each item in this category.

Next, look for those important matters that you would *like* to get to if you can. Mark those items with a B.

Finally, select the items on your list that can wait or are optional. Those you mark with the letter C.

Now go through each letter group and prioritize those tasks. For example, your most important A task you will designate as A-1. Your next most important A task is A-2.

Do the same with the Bs and Cs.

Finally, put a time estimate next to each task. For example, if your A-1 task is to complete a report that's due on Friday, and you know it's going to take you about two hours, put a 2 next to it. I put my letters at the beginning and my time estimates at the end, like this:

*A-1 Finish the report on dental floss distribution. 2*

*A-2 Start research on new sources of dental floss. 1.5*

All this doesn't take long to do once you're used to it, and the benefits are immediate. You won't have to guess what to schedule for the week, or what task to tackle next during the day. You'll have the plan all set out for you.

Be somewhat flexible. If some urgent task pops up, find the right place for it in your list and adjust the other items.

Make a new list every week, eliminating those tasks that no longer apply and adding whatever new ones you need.

### 3. Take advantage of your best hour of the day

Everybody has one hour of the day where they feel the most creative, energetic, sharp, and good looking. For many people that comes in the morning. For me it's about half an hour into my day, after I've started on that first cup of coffee. I like to wake up early, when it's still dark, and start the coffee going for my wife who is still snoozing quietly away. I then take my cup and go to the computer.

Find your own favorite hour. It might be at night when the kids are finally asleep. Or maybe it's when you're at Starbucks at noon and the espresso starts to kick in.

Whatever it is, determine to take full advantage of that hour. Put your head down and work. Do not check your phone or your email. Do not go on Twitter or Facebook. Do not pass Go. Do not collect $200.

You can probably get three times more done in this one hour than at any other hour during your day.

### 4. Do one thing at a time

Forget multitasking when you work. Put full concentration on the task at hand.

What you're trying to get to is a sense of *Flow*, as described by psychologist Mihaly Csíkszentmihalyi in his book of the same name (*Flow: The Psychology of Optimal Experience*; Harper Perennial, 2008). This is a state of deep, immersive attention. When it happens, you are at your best, mentally and creatively. You know this in part because time seems to speed up.

Another term for this state is being in "the zone." You get it from doing just one thing at a time.

### 5. Take short breaks

You can't efficiently concentrate on something indefinitely. Studies show that if you focus hard for about fifty minutes, then take a ten-minute break, your efficiency will optimize.

If you are at a workplace with a Lumbergh watching you (see the movie *Office Space*), you'll need to find a way to rest your brain for a few minutes. It's not hard to do.

Sit up straight in your chair, close your eyes, and take five long, slow breaths. As you do, count down from five. 5-4-3-2-1. Then slowly open your eyes and take one more deep breath. If you can wear headphones and listen to some soft or classical music (or ocean sounds) try that for a few minutes. Imagine you're sitting on a nice beach. Smell the suntan lotion.

Take your full lunch hour. And don't take it eating at your desk.

### 6. Take a real rest one day a week

Use one whole day per week for creative leisure. Read. Learn a new subject. Get courses from The Teaching Company (an outstanding resource!). But also this: Use part of the day for pure loafing. That's right. We live in such a hurry-up world. It's possible to fill every second with some sort of activity. Down time is almost unheard of. We can be Tweeting or Facebooking, texting, playing Angry Birds or any of an infinite number of games. If you don't learn to shut out the noise for at least part of your week, you'll be more tired and just plain disagreeable than you otherwise might be. And we have to live with you. So loaf.

### 7. Use Google Reader to quickly go through relevant material

Using Google Reader enables you to pick blogs and feeds that impact your life and skim the headlines. Don't be sucked into the trap of reading everything.

If you get printed magazines or newsletters, go quickly over the contents and tear out the articles you want to read. Save those for down time, when you're waiting in line and the like. Toss the rest of the magazine in the can.

### 8. Set aside time for email and social media

Do not approach these tasks haphazardly. Schedule time for them or they'll suck the time out of you.

### 9. Learn how to power nap

I take a power nap each day during my zombie phase, which is for me, 2–4 p.m. I put my feet up on my desk, or go lie down, and am out for 15 to 20 minutes. That's it. You can learn to do this. It takes a little time, but your body will soon cooperate. I estimate I get an hour and a half of more productive time in the evening if I take a power nap in the afternoon.

After your power nap, drink a big glass of water and down a few almonds or walnuts with raisins.

### 10.  Throughout the day ask, "What's the best use of my time right now?"

Even if it's only for thirty seconds at a time, get in this habit. If you save a few minutes, those minutes accumulate.

### 11.  Make TV your slave, not the other way around

DVR news programs so you can whip through them instead of watching them live. Consider doing the same for sports, so you can fast-forward during time outs and commercials. Make a game of seeing how much TV you can do without.

### 12.  Reward yourself when you have reached a significant milestone

When I finish a manuscript I like to take a full day off and go on a literary goof. There are used bookstores in L.A. I like, so I'll start there, browse the shelves, pick up that Cornell Woolrich I've been missing, or add to my collection of 50's paperback originals. I might just go to a park or the beach, put out a chair and read. That night, I'll take my wife to one of our favorite places for dinner. You simply have to enjoy the journey or what's the point of it all?

### 13.  Eat a light lunch so you don't get draggy in the afternoon

Salad. Tuna. Chicken. Fruit.
Drink plenty of water.

### 14.  Learn how to skim books

This is a little harder to do in the age of the e-reader. I prefer printed nonfiction so I can quickly scan the table of contents and chapters and individual pages. The secret to skimming is to create questions you want the book to answer. That way, you're not so concerned with reading cover to cover. You can read looking only for the relevant passages. No law says you have to read every word of every book.

### 15.  Always have something to read for "waiting" times

At the very least, have something queued up on your smart phone.

### 16.  Master 80/20 thinking

Recall that, generally, eighty percent of your results come from twenty percent of your activities. Or the other way around, twenty percent of what you do is going to determine eighty percent of your result. If, for example, you have a list of ten items on your current To Do list, two of them are going to be the most important tasks to perform.

Identify them and do them first.

### 17. Delegate as much as you can

If there is any way to get someone else to perform lower level tasks for you, even if it costs you a little money, hire them. Save your own time for the most important things you have to do your own sweet self.

### 18. Handle each correspondence only once

Be it paper or email correspondence, deal with it immediately. If it doesn't demand a response, don't respond.

### 19. Learn the art of "snatching" time

You can prepare to use "off" times productively. In your car, instead of always listening to music, listen to a self-study course. When you go to the doctor or dentist, bring a project with you. When you fly somewhere, plan to use eighty percent of the flight time doing something productive, not playing games or watching movies.

For long flights I always bring something to edit, something to read, and my computer to write on.

I get a window seat so I won't have anyone piling over me to get to the bathroom.

### 20. Find something higher to live for

Life is not about you alone. It's about relationships and giving and making the world a better place. The happiest people on earth are those who find a way to give something back. Be one of those people.

---

James Scott Bell, *How to Make a Living as a Writer* (Woodland Hills, CA: Compendium Press, 2014), 229-230.

••• Visit jamesscottbell.com •••

## Assignments

1. Look at how you plan the specifics of your writing life. Franklin Planner? Scrap paper? Computer calendar? App? Assess how your planning tools work for you, or against you.

2. Pay attention to how you spend your days. What do you waste time on? What time savers do you utilize? When is your top writing time? Plan out your day in 15-minute increments to see how you might work in more writing time.

3. How do you take time to rest? Daily? Weekly? Monthly? Build in a 30-minute rest each day, at least a half day of relaxation each week, and a day-long retreat each month. What keeps you from rest?

4.  Assess how you spend your time on social media. Do you let Facebook take up an hour each day? Get sucked into Pinterest? Set aside the time you need to spend posting/reposting on social media, then stick to that time.

5.  List five tasks you can delegate to a writer's helper, those with whom you live, or service people. Tasks can include research, house cleaning, cooking meals, or running errands. If this is difficult for you, ponder how you might relinquish your need for control.

# Acknowledgments

This book is the product of many. Without the help of the many professionals who offered their time and expertise, *Christian Publishing 101* wouldn't exist. Thank you many times over for your willingness to let me ask question after question.

Thank you also to my writers group, The Guild, for their unwavering encouragement, commiseration, and fortifying strength in times of stress and discouragement. They gave me the gimlet eye when I needed it and a shoulder to cry on when I needed that just as much.

The members of the Breathe Planning Committee, all friends and writing allies, offered me the gift of friendship and like-mindedness as we put together the Breathe Christian Writers Conference.

And to my family: my parents who let me bunk at their empty house over the summer for writing weekends, and my husband and children, who know how to make corn dogs and other junk food, buy pizza, and eat oatmeal to keep themselves fed while I write.

Also in the Credo Publishing University series . . .

# WRITE WITH EXCELLENCE 201:

## A lighthearted guide to the serious matter of writing well— for Christian authors, editors, and students

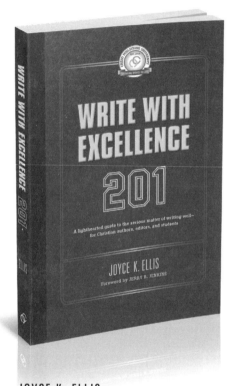

- three major sections covering grammar, punctuation, and style
- forty-six chapters on everything from defibrillating verbs to avoiding apostrophe abuse
- quizzes at the end of each chapter to apply knowledge to one's own writing
- lots of humor, actually making grammar fun.

If you are at the beginning of your writing career, you are fortunate to hold this book in your hands. Joyce K. Ellis's brilliant, informative, and accessible book will save you hundreds of hours of learning everything the hard way. If you are well along in your career, this book is guaranteed to teach you things you didn't know before. Either way, I advise you to keep this book on your shelf, right between your dictionary and your thesaurus. It's that good.

**ROBERT HUDSON,** author, *The Christian Writer's Manual of Style: 4th Edition*

**JOYCE K. ELLIS** has been writing, editing, and teaching for more than forty years, during which she has published hundreds of articles and more than a dozen fiction and nonfiction books. Ellis has earned a Gold Medallion Award for *The One-Minute Bible for Kids* and numerous awards for her magazine articles.

Available on Amazon.com and Barnesandnoble.com
Retail Price: $19.99 USD | $26.99 CAD